MW00881696

The Malibu Cookbook

A Memoir By THE GODMOTHER OF MALIBU

Illustrations By Valerie Titus Parker....

Bloomington, IN Milton Keynes, UK

authorHOUSE

AuthorHouse™
1663 Liberty Drive, Suite 200
Bloomington, IN 47403
www.authorhouse.com
Phone: 1-800-839-8640

AuthorHouse™ UK Ltd.
500 Avebury Boulevard
Central Milton Keynes, MK9 2BE
www.authorhouse.co.uk
Phone: 08001974150

First published by AuthorHouse 11/9/2007

ISBN: 978-1-4259-1434-9 (sc)
ISBN: 978-1-4259-1435-6 (hc)

Printed in the United States of America
Bloomington, Indiana

This book is printed on acid-free paper.

AS YOU WALK AND EAT
AND TRAVEL,
BE WHERE YOU ARE.
OTHERWISE YOU WILL MISS
MOST OF YOUR LIFE.

—BUDDHA

Preface
By Ali Mac Graw

I don't know exactly how long it has been that I have known the Godmother, but it feels like forever. Maybe that's because we are both New Yorkers at heart, and my friend Dolores is nothing if not the poster person for New York City, and the Bronx. But however many years it is since I started bringing my then-little son to the Godmother—after school, a ritual—it has always felt like a kind of "home" to me. Marlys makes the kind of food that I love and was brought up on: clean, fresh, basic and delicious. And Dolores—well, her energy and presence, her huge heart, her "godmother-ness," have always made for the best kind of life force imaginable.

I remember those early days in Malibu at the Godmother (the tiny place at Cross Creek); I stopped there virtually every afternoon with a carload of hungry little after-school boys, including my own. They all ate that delicious gourmet food as though they were on their way to the electric chair, and I remember my son' famous one-liner after each ingredient-specific order: "Charge it to my mom."

And I remember all the great lunches I ate, either at one of the small, dark-green café tables or as take-away to my rented beach house. And there were wonderful dinners too, packed up to go back home, with masses of red wine. In those days I loved to drink wine, and Dolores would always have a new bottle for me to "try" as if I knew a single thing about wine, ever.

But the thing I remember most is the laughter, each and every time. Marlys, and later her beautiful daughter Valerie would be upstairs preparing perfect food for an impossible number of meals, and Dolores would be downstairs, taking orders, organizing, talking to everyone in Malibu—and above all, laughing that great great laugh that made you just want to be at the Godmother all day. Yes, there were some "celebrities" but what I remember most is that the people who consistently frequented the Godmother were just plain nice—and real. Dolores has a terrific nose for bullshit—New York street smarts, I guess—and the people who are still, to this day, the Godmother's loyal customers are, for the most part, like a kind of faintly-connected, real family. I think we all felt safe and welcome there, like going back to a happy home.

I know that the annual Christmas decorating at the shop was a major part of my own holiday, and I miss it. There was fabulous food being prepared, a hundred impossible, last minute orders for enormous feasts, which Marlys managed with her usual serenity. Downstairs, Dolores held high-energy court, while Valerie and I packed dozens of baskets for gifts, and worked on the Christmas tree. All of our beloved dogs were invited, too. And our friend Debe supplied an extraordinary electric train which went round and round the tree, bearing gift bottles of Italian olive oil, homemade grapefruit jam, and whatever other special goodies had been prepared. She packaged and lifted and decorated with great style. It was magic, like somehow going back to a safe and memorable childhood.

So there was all this divine food, all that high energy and all that laughter. My darling friend Dolores was the magnet for all of this, and she and her family and friends have managed to keep the Godmother special and vital for all these years. Their "new" place is perfect, and the food continues to astound. Nowadays there are even more huge and complicated weddings and parties to be catered to perfection; it is an incredibly successful business, and I am so proud of my long-time friend. And I suppose that the Malibu of today has delivered even more "celebrities" to the Godmother, many of them asking for their favorite soba noodles or Tomato Bisque, Tiramisu— whatever. But for me, the Godmother will always be about good, classic food, whirlwind energy, no nonsense and laughter. So enjoy all these wonderful recipes. But remember that there are still missing ingredients: Dolores (the Godmother), Marlys and Valerie. This book is as close as many of you will get to the Godmother of Malibu—but you'll definitely get the idea!!!

THE GODMOTHER'S COOKBOOK

We know the Godmother as Dolores,
Her Italian last name's too much for us;
But she's a legend here in Malibu
For the haute cuisine she serves to you;
There's no question that she outrates
All other culinary greats.

Jacques Pepin in his proudest day,
Not even France's Escoffier,
Could ever match her gourmet dishes,
As for Wolfgang Puck, he only wishes!
The chefs at Beau Rivage and Sage
Were once the overwhelming rage.

You had to stand in line at Granitas
For pizza, pilaf and frittatas;
And Tra Di Noi if you spoke Venetian,
Saddle Peak Lodge for wild game;
But Godmother has put them all to shame!

The Malibu Racquet Club is her venue,
Where one dines from a Three Star menu;
In this alfresco setting you must be able
To duck tennis balls bouncing off your table.
But there is much, much more to praise

At Dolores's place on sunny days.
You should know that Dolores also caters,
Supplies all you require, even the waiters;
For weddings, birthdays, bar mitzvahs, too,
Count on her to bring the feast to you.
Wherever you live, up the hills or over the surf,
Malibu is known as Dolores's turf.

By Malibu's own beloved poet extraordinaire, Roy Ringer.....
(Sadly Roy died in May, 2007, most likely penning another
poignant poem to send back to us. He will be missed.

PROLOGUE

IF YOU'RE BORED IN
NEW YORK,
IT'S YOUR OWN FAULT.

—MYRNA LOY

I am a New Yorker; I have all of the characteristics, real or exaggerated, good or bad, that are New York, like a hair trigger temper and absolutely NO PATIENCE. I usually let everyone know what I think. The wise ones don't even ask anymore. Those who know me know how vocal I am about food: mediocre restaurants, fast-foods, and just plain bad food; I just can't keep my mouth shut. So I decided to do something about it and let my friends off the hook: write a cookbook and tell all who read it what I think. Maybe no one will care, but at least my friends and family don't have to listen to me anymore.

I've been the route of publishing giants, but they wanted much more than I was willing to give. For instance, Doubleday wanted "scoops" on celebrities. I told them where to put it. This was not easy as I sat in a wood-paneled room in their New York office. Here was everything I had hoped would happen. A conglomerate was interested in publishing my book, and yet I wasn't about to give them "scoops" on anyone. What they didn't know is that I didn't have any scoops on anyone but I wasn't about to give them any information that I considered private on my clients and friends.

The book is about me, my family, my friends, the many twists and turns in the road I choose to follow in this lifetime and my passion for food, and how all this affected the past twenty-seven plus years at The Godmother. If the big publishers wanted more, they could buy a subscription to People magazine.

I couldn't believe that they wouldn't just want to hear from an Italian raised in the Bronx who was living so far from where it all began and doing it well.. Here I was in Malibu, California, the envy of all and enjoying such a colorful life as The Godmother of Malibu —what other celebrity has that kind of longevity? Who was more qualified than me to write a memoir? I guess they were wondering who would really care. Who knows?....they wanted guarantees; I could only deliver a story....I know my friends and family would care but maybe that's not enough for a "best seller".

I'm from a family that could only cook mouth-watering foods, and I was born and raised in a city where if you spin around and stop suddenly at a place that served food, it would most likely be a fairly decent place to eat, even if it looks like a "greasy spoon". Dining out is one of the great pleasures of living or visiting New York. It is and always will be a world class restaurant town.

The Bronx was and still is unique. It's a world of wonders...for kids especially. In the summer, we either went to the Botanical Gardens, rolling in the grass until our legs were green, or the Bronx Zoo, playing in the elephant house or with my favorites, the penguins, with their little black and white suits. We played stick ball in the street every day and games such as "kick the can" and "ring a leeveo" and if we were really lucky, went to Yankee Stadium a lot.

When we got hungry, we made rock piles in the empty lot on our block, lit a fire, threw potatoes into the flames and twenty minutes later, we were eating mouth watering potatoes, smothered in warm butter borrowed from our parents refrigerators. Most afternoons, when I went into dinner, (dinner for me was always 4pm because my father worked nights and he had to sleep at least six hours before he left for work at 11pm) I smelled like charred wood. My mother pleaded, "Stop with the fire already, you'll get burned." I'd jump up and down, before going home, hoping to get rid of the fire smell so she wouldn't be upset, but she was a smart cookie with a great nose.

Little did I know then, that growing up in the Bronx outfitted me for the world and especially Southern California; where what you think you see, you really don't.

The Bronx was such an incredible place to be born and raised.

For one thing, The Bronx is the only borough of New York with a "the" in front of it. The Bronx has the largest park in New York City, the 2,765-acre Pelham Bay Park, where you can still walk safely, well, at least during the day.

The nineteen-foot tall statue of Abraham Lincoln at the Lincoln Memorial in Washington was carved by the Piccirilli brothers, in a studio on East 142nd Street in the Bronx. Every year Bronx Week is held, It's the longest running event of its kind in the five boroughs.

This incredibly, unique part of New York was quite possibly visited by the Virgin Mary, reportedly the mother of God, in 1945 when a nine-year old boy swore that he saw the Virgin Mary in a vision; thousands lined the street outside his home. Life magazine called it "The Bronx Miracle". Then, President Harry Truman decided to follow the vision; never said whether or not he saw the Virgin himself.

President John F. Kennedy drove by and waved to Bronxites in 1962. I was there and waved back. I'm sure he noticed. I yelled louder than anyone else.

Pope John Paul 11 came in 1977, and in the last few years, President Bill Clinton decided to make the Bronx his working home which is just another blessing and something worth celebrating for all its residents. And the best thing of course about The Bronx is that the greatest team in the history of baseball is located there.... "the Bronx Bombers".

The Bronx managed to raise kids who were a lot like me. Thank God we didn't all settle in Malibu. Mouthy, independent, carefree with few fears. Most of us were very black and white, not always right but black and white. Some people call it typical New York behavior. I call it sense of self behavior. I'm proud of it too..

You had to be a survivor to make it through the streets of the Bronx. Public school, high school, college; trying to get on the subway at rush hour, trying to cross a street like Boston Post Road where my high school, Evander Childs is located...surviving as latch-key kids because our parents had to work.—Everything was challenging, but we didn't give it much thought, because everyone did it. We didn't need much therapy to survive our childhoods either...You just did it.

In New York, I didn't seem to drive people nuts with my strong stance on everything, from how to slice onions to what good pizza is, but here I do.

People in sunny California not only want to look and sound good, but they want to be liked at any cost. My God, that takes a lot of work. People don't say what they are really thinking or feeling. Playing it safe is a huge stress-builder. Fear is a killer.

I don't think you should ever hurt anyone's feelings if you can possibly avoid it, but you must be honest with yourself and with others.

People deserve to know who you are. In the wonderful Broadway musical, 'Mame', the character Mame, reveals her true feelings, a bit disguised, when she says."I can't begin to tell you what I think of your home", which she really disliked. (more about Mame later) It says it all without saying it all. In New York, people, for the most part don't give a damn if you're different. It never mattered what color or what religion you were. Not in my neighborhood anyway. You were a New Yorker, everybody was in the same boat.

I learned early on how different this was in other parts of the country when I married a Marine pilot and left New York for the first time, to join him at the Marine base at Cherry Point, North Carolina.

I arrived in New Bern, North Carolina, the small town near the base, dressed in a very sophisticated and beautiful beige wool dress with large dark brown buttons down the length of the dress that my friend Dian's mother, Henrietta made me, (remember when you could get your clothes made by someone with talent and it didn't cost thousands???) brown high heels and matching bag (looking very New York chic), I boarded the bus that would take me to the base and did what I always do when I get on the bus. I walked to the back and sat down. The gentlemen sitting next to me was elderly and well-dressed. I smiled and he returned the smile. With all seats filled, the bus doors closed but the bus didn't move. I didn't think much of it because rumor had it that the South was a bit more layed back than New York (to say the least). I was resigned to go with the flow. What the hell, this was my first adventure outside of New York. Finally, the bus driver yells "young lady, please come and sit up front". I thanked him and said "I'm fine". After a few seconds, he repeated himself with an added "move now!" I was appalled! How could anyone talk to me that way? "I'll sit where I want to sit, I thought. "What a weird-o", I whispered to my seat companion, who immediately turned and said "if you don't move we will be here all day". I saw the anguish on his face and moved forward immediately. The bus took off.

I was told that I was lucky. They tar and feather "northerners" for less. It was an unwritten rule of the South, blacks sit in the back, whites sit up front. How primitive, I thought. How awful for people to be subjected to this kind of cruelty because of the color of their skin. That was my first, certainly not my last experience with the stench of prejudice.

I'm not kidding when I said I don't care if I'm liked or not. As long as I am doing the best I can possibly do, never wanting to hurt anyone with my honesty and directness.

This is indeed a very New York characteristic; the one where you don't act on the basis of what other people will think of you. This made the opening of The Godmother of Malibu seem like a very natural thing to do.

I knew from the moment I could talk, I was not cut out for the diplomatic corps. As much as I think that at times it would've made my life a little easier, if I didn't offer my opinion so often. I couldn't keep my mouth shut. My mother, a truly wonderful soul, warned me repeatedly "Sweetheart, maybe a little less opinion."

When I hear anyone with that distinct New York accent, in California or Egypt, I feel like I've met a friend. During the past several years, more Malibuites are sounding like New Yorkers...maybe

I'm rubbing off on them finally after so many years living in this wonderful town.

I have been a New York Yankee fan since I was three years old. so they tell me. I will be a New York Yankee fan until I die....and then we'll see.My devotion to them will never change despite my anger when they don't play good ball.

When I was thirteen years old (hard for me to believe that I was ever thirteen years old), I was at Yankee Stadium watching a game between the Yanks and the Boston Red Sox's (our scorned rivals) which we won as usual. It was always a thrill for us to sneak from our usual cheap seats in the bleachers, to the expensive box seats around the eighth inning when the guards could care less....

As Joe Di Maggio raced across center field to catch the last fly ball of the game, I jumped onto the field, from our 'new seats' and started running towards him. I have no idea to this day what possessed me. The cops were pretty easy going in those days because the Yankees were Gods, and they weren't concerned about some kid running into the ball field, especially SOME GIRL because they knew that nobody would ever think of hurting a Yankee.

DiMaggio saw me coming and just kept running towards the dugout.

"Hi kid," he said as he approached me. My knees buckled but I turned quickly and stretched out my arms and my fingers touched his jersey, right on his famed number 5.

I swore that I was NEVER going to wash those fingers. I kept them hidden in my pocket for days so my Mother wouldn't see the adhesive tape around them. Funny how smart Mothers are. Only when my fingers started to swell and turn blue did she finally say, "Stop already with that tape and wash your hand before it falls off."

Sadly I headed towards the sink.

I love New York because it has Hebrew National hot dogs served from suspicious-looking carts. The first bite into those hotdogs brings pure ambrosia, the skin pops and those luscious juices spill down your throat around the Guldens Mustard...and surprisingly, no one I ever knew got sick from eating one of them. I love New York because it has the Metropolitan Museum of Art, the Metropolitan Opera, Lincoln Center, Carnegie Hall, the Hayden Planetarium, the Museum of Natural History, the Guggenheim, all of Broadway, and real Jewish delis where if the counterman smiles at you, you feel like you've been officially welcomed.

I love New York because it has Central Park, the Bronx Zoo, Little Italy, Chinatown, where the best Chinese food in the entire world awaits your chopsticks...... the bohemian history of Greenwich Village, and Tiffany's, where you probably could still have a Cracker Jack Toy-Ring engraved. (Like the one George Peppard and Audrey Hepburn had engraved in the movie *Breakfast at Tiffany's*)

I love New York because I don't live there any longer.

There are so many people to thank, an endless list of customers and friends. This book would resemble the New York telephone directory if I listed each of you separately... You know who you are. If I listed names and I forgot someone, it would be ungodmotherly. So as Tiny Tim said in Charles Dickens' "Christmas Carol". "Thank you one and all".

However, my deep appreciation must be given to a some special ladies who are no longer with us and who made a huge difference in my life. My world was so much richer when they were here and is now so much less without them.

Each of these women in their own way was strong, independent and groundbreaking. They were role models for me, whether they were family, friends, or clients, or all of the above. Strong, smart, savvy; caring "Godmother" type people.

Mary Marsami D'Eletto, my mom
Marlys Mcfarlane, our grandma
Wilma Billie Gay Estes Hall, Godmother III
Audrey Schuessler Militano, One of a kind
Gemma Rivellino Fazio, my aunt
Elsie Rivellino Ippolito, my aunt
Teresa Rivellino, my grandma
Maria D'Eletto, my grandma
Henrietta Norton, my "other mother"
Betty D'Eletto, my aunt
Emma Chiappa..my aunt

And dear friends and Malibuites
Dottie Irwin
Margaret Dixie Jewison
Carol Tannenbaum Rapf
Tita Cooley
Cordelia Rodrick
Amanda Dunne
Mickey Ziffren
Shirley Courage

As you turn the pages, I hope you feel the warmth and magic of these years, and that you actually feel as though you were with us, at The Godmother, tasting the food, drinking the wine, soaking up the ambience in that Spanish décor courtyard watching all of those characters who sipped a cappuccino or hummed over chicken pasta.

Yes, I have a big mouth and I'm fun. Yes, I enjoy people. Yes, I am the personality behind The Godmother but the truth is I don't cook...I stopped cooking on May 17, 1980 when we opened The Godmother.

I taught Marlys a few basic recipes, important ones like marinara sauce, which if you didn't know, is the key to all good cooking, Italian or not. Once she got it (and boy was she was a quick learner), I traded in my sauce pan for a "band stand" and she took off.

In my very judgmental opinion, she became one of the finest chefs on the West Coast.

I, on the other hand, became THE GODMOTHER, with the charm and charisma of a movie star. I greeted the rich and famous, the poor and unknown. I try to tell people I don't cook but they don't believe me. I'm very righteous about food and I know this gets a little tiresome for the poor souls who have to listen to my ramblings at times.

But I grew up in The Bronx in a household of Italian immigrants, where taste and tradition mattered above all else. So I wanted to relive my childhood, as all of us do at some point in our adult lives, and what better way than with The Godmother? With an unlimitied reservoir of energy and desire, I knew exactly what I wanted to offer. It had to be damn good...it had to be not only healthy, and beautifully presented but it had to taste like "Heaven's Food on Earth".... Tall order!

Marlys delivered.

Everything I obsessed over she was able to create, and because of her God-given skills, she removed my neurosis about food on a daily basis. She has been the "architect" of our kitchen for all of these years.

Never taking even a backyard cooking class, except the ones I've gave her on the run, she has designed and orchestrated some of the finest menus, always maintaining integrity in her cooking. Remarkable since it's a long way from her profession as a registered nurse. Her consistency in delivering this quality of food to the community of Malibu over such a long period of time has never been matched by any restaurant, catering service or personal chef...No one comes close to her talents. Angels,? I wonder!!

The Godmother is one of only two of the <u>oldest food establishments</u> in Malibu under the same ownership. The other is an outdoor market called John's Garden featuring fresh salads, sandwiches and wooden stands bulging with seasonal fruits and vegetables. Coincidentially, John's Garden also started in a van.

Billie Gay, who never got a chance to see the continued success of the Godmother, (she died in 1986) was the "general contractor." She agreed to support my then outrageous idea of creating The Godmother with all the nearly impossible challenges we faced. She gave us the chance for the dream, by opening her heart and her checkbook.

What I brought to the table was the ability to listen to people, and to care; to understand what they wanted and to respect and acknowledge their likes and dislikes; to make their events, my event; to make them trust me. I'm like a food therapist, without the couch. If someday, I decide to invest in the couch, a whole new career could be awaiting me.

In 1980, Valerie was twelve years old. Reluctantly, she worked for the first Godmother, along with her brother Duane who was fifteen years old. The first Godmother was a huge, shiny new catering van. Val couldn't have cared less that it was new and could possibly be an adventure. She felt awkward and I think in the beginning she was embarrassed. Malibu is a small town and driving around in a big white catering van was a bit obvious and "weird" to most twelve year olds. I think it made her uncomfortable in front of her school chums. Most of the time, Duane took it in stride, because he got to drive the van occasionally, especially when we needed to back it up... I could never back it up... who could see that far back there?

He loved the challenge of what the van experiences brought to us every day. He was 'our guy' for whenever guys are needed. Repairs, errands, deliveries, restocking. They both worked after school and on weekends. They were the very first (unpaid) Godmother employees. Food was prepared at our home and carried into and out of the van every day. Coffee urns had to be scrubbed every night. The actual cooking of the food was done in the van. It's kitchen was more up-to-date than our own kitchen.

When we moved into a more permanent location on Cross Creek Road, they were a lot more willing to help in any way they could. Eventually, Duane moved to Sandpoint, Idaho. Val stayed with us after she graduated from UCLA. She taught herself the art of food design, and with her very special gifts, always made the presentation of food very, dramatically attractive and appealing. The food cases at the shop were the talk of the town, certainly like nothing Malibu had ever seen before. The food always looked so tempting, but the real surprise was in the taste because the foods were actually as delicious as they looked.

The Godmother has worked so well for the past quarter-century because our small family fit the pieces of the puzzle in different ways to make it whole.

Valerie is a lovely woman today, married to Bruce, a well-respected Malibu chiropractor and one of my angels for his patience with my lack of any computer sense. They are parents to an incredibly precious little girl named Kailani Kea. Hopefully Valerie will carry the torch of The Godmother into the future. With her artistic talents, charm, tenacity, and her uncompromising value system, she will always be the poster girl for The Godmother.

Duane, is a handsome, quiet, self-assured man with enormous integrity and many talents who returned to live in Malibu several years ago.

Although he's in another profession, he is always there for us in case the stove stops working the day before Thanksgiving when we've trying to roast 49 turkeys or the walk-in refrigerator decides to quit in the middle of a busy lunch hour. Duane is married to the lovely Rebecca, who has enriched our family. She is a strong animal rights activist.

Life sometimes is pretty special. We are very fortunate and grateful for the many blessings we have received.

Our success wasn't accidental. However, it happened because of guardian angels (always watching out for us) hard work, talent, and good luck; dedication to our family, our friends, very loyal clients and our devoted staff—that all adds up to a very happy and full life.

We are here today also because of our present staff and those who have moved on to other food havens around the world, after giving us so much of their talents. We've learned so much from the many people who passed through The Godmother. They are all extraordinary people. Without them, we could never have experienced such longevity and success.

A Special Thanks to...

DENISE RITCHIE who was one of the first to walk through our wooden screen doors the week we opened; she entered The Godmother world and hasn't left.

She was looking for food to fit one of her many strange diets. She is a dear friend and today eats like the rest of us. But that took a lot of work.

In the early days, she was married and living 'comfortably" on Zumirez road, a very high-end neighborhood in Malibu (that's an oxymoron for sure, but there are some low, medium and high ends to Malibu). She and her then-husband were always looking for a 'fix' to their alleged health and weight problems. We cooked some God-awful stuff for them...not necessarily bad tasting but awful combinations that were supposed to clean out your digestive system. These were the years when people ate a lot of meat. The idea of a no animal and no dairy diet (remember, this is 1980-81) was as extreme as tanning salons. Vegetarianism was considered a disease rather than a way of life. Denise and her husband were vegetarian for lack of a better word.

With our help, they began a whole new trend of foods. We developed some very special and still-used recipes One of the most popular, which I personally disliked, was Tofu Lasagna. Not because it tasted bad, but because REAL Italians don't use tofu.

Experimenting didn't come cheap. Food and labor costs were high, but Denise and her then husband never complained. This was a very endearing characteristic which solidified a lasting relationship in such a creative yet risky business. It turns out, strange as the concept was, we were the first restaurant/café in Malibu to offer a vegetarian menu, thanks to Denise and her families strange needs.

Denise is a gifted writer. She and her husband, Randy, have written many screenplays. They're stuff is good. I'm always amazed at their abilities to create such colorful and clever tales. Someday, someone in this town may get sick and tired of most of the schlock that is currently produced and turn one of their scripts into a movie that will be worth spending twelve bucks to see. In the meantime, they currently own and operate one of the most successful landscaping businesses in Southern California.

Denise welcomed the challenge of the cookbook. It got her away from the screenplays for a while. We went through many, many revisions, and hundreds of pages until we hit on the formula which got me through the stacks of boxes I'd piled throughout the years, full of notes and scraps of paper. She made sense out of what I thought were neurotic ramblings from a bizarre mind. She became my editor and my conscience. This book would not have begun without her.

AND FINALLY MANDY...

For three consecutive years, we catered a cocktail party, hosted by Malibuites Dick and Elsa Gary, for Southern California parents of students attending Middlebury College in Vermont. Their daughter, Amanda, was an undergraduate studying among other things, Italian, in this very prestigious East Coast Ivy-league school.

It was a well-planned event for all to meet and discuss their kids, and of course enjoy good food.

I always looked forward to seeing the Gary's.

When Amanda graduated, the parties naturally ceased. At this point I had never met the face that was the reason for these parties.

A few years later, when I was planning a trip to Italy, one of my favorites places, I saw an ad in our local newspaper for Italian lessons. Could I get to sound like Sophia Loren in three weeks?

Truly a small world it is! The "teacher" turned out to be the Gary daughter, Amanda (or Mandy, as I call her). She had recently returned from a year in Italy.

We meet and it's love at first sight. As a young, bright, eager, adventurous woman, she travels the globe and uses the world as her stage, squeezing every ounce out of her experiences so that she can someday be not only a published but a very successful writer. I have no doubt that all that will happen.

She speaks Italian like a native; it was evident from day one that I was never going to master Italian like she has especially in time for my trip, or most probably ever in my lifetime.

I decided to put the Italian lessons aside and use Mandy's incredible command of English and structure, to help me finish the book. She jumped right in and actually welcomed the challenge of placing literally thousands of pages in the right order. She picked up where Denise left off.

She typed this "damn cookbook" (as she lovingly refers to it,) 'hundreds' of times. It was as if she too had lived with this for ten years. Her suggestions were smart, and her knowledge of the English language is a testament to her fine education. I hope her parents take great comfort when they read this acknowledgement that they did spend their money at Middlebury College wisely.

I was resisting writing the end of the cookbook. Maybe I had grown so fond of it that I didn't want to share it with anyone. It was kind of like an old friend leaving on a long, long trip. I didn't want to say goodbye.

Just before she left on yet another overseas adventure, Mandy put the book in order one more time, and in desperation left a note on the front cover...in her own special language, one I could understand very clearly: "You, me lady, are in bidnez...FINISH THE BOOK."

Without her, it NEVER would've been finished.

On one of her returns, the first thing out of her mouth was "NO, NO, I AM NOT TYPING IT AGAIN!!!." My charm and a good Godmother lunch won out, and she did indeed type it yet one more time....Mandy will always be one of the special people in my life.

THE BIG BIG DISCLAIMER...........

THIS BOOK is very unorthodox ESPECIALLY AS A COOKBOOK...

The whole writing thing has been a process which has given me a crash course on the publishing business. For instance, I learned that publishers of fine cookbooks, have very strict requirements for listing a recipe. Ironicially, those recipes in these good-looking coffee-table-type cookbooks don't always work out despite their 'requirements'...

When a recipe fails, 99% of the time it's the recipe and not the 'cook' ...Sometimes the slightest adjustment in the recipe or failure to include all of the amounts correctly (very common) throws everything off. But are you really going to call the publishing company or return the book to the store????. Of course not. It's so much easier to blame yourself.

We've tested hundreds of recipes through the years and found that their specific requirements are sometimes not so specific.

So from the start I want you to know the gamble you're undertaking. We've ignored the traditional testing of any recipe... we simply list the ingredients and tell you how to do it. This is how we do it at the Godmother and we've done it this way for over a quarter of a century.

They work for us, and with a few exceptions, (Tomato Bisque and those other recipes that came in dreams), will work for you...

With the few exceptions noted, all of the recipes in this cookbook are original Godmother creations...

part one

IT'S THE PROCESS THAT'S IMPORTANT

—ROBERT ALTMAN
PRODUCER/DIRECTOR

FRIDAY NIGHTS

Josie was my Godmother. She was young and beautiful; she was my Mother's best friend. They met when everyone had apartments at 3315 Cruger Avenue in the Bronx, which was my first home. It was a large building with about thirty apartments, separate like condos. And it was uptown from where my grandparents had immigrated thirty years before. This building was my first contact with 'celebrity' (as told to me a thousand times). Sylvia Sidney, who was as famous then as Madonna is today, was the daughter of Jewish immigrants from Russia and she visited often with her Mother who had an apartment on the same floor as ours. The building was loaded with immigrants; Jews and Italians and they all had the same hand movements and talked the same "language".

My mother swore (remember this is from a mother's perspective), that Sylvia just "loved me so," thought I was so adorable and loved to push me in my stroller whenever she visited.

I am sure this is where I got my first love of films. Sylvia's first film was in 1927, Broadway Nights, and her last film Mars Attack, in 1996 made her one of the very lasting stars of her day.

It was the 1940's and people were struggling with the long aftermath of the Depression. War clouds hung over the country. Unemployment was the highest it had been in history. It was a period in which people leaned on each other. Families were very important and stayed very close. How ever did they survive without big screen television, cell phones, Macs, Ipods and Blackberries?

Sunday was my favorite day of the week because we had dinner at my grandparents every Sunday...no matter what. Their home was old, but big and warm with delicious smells coming from the kitchen. It felt very safe for a little kid.

My grandma was a firm believer that we go where God sends us, and that there are no accidents. She was very pious and believed in Angels. Not just the kind that flutter around, but special people who come into our lives and whisper God's plan into our ears. Grandma said Josie was one of those Angels.

Most Italians believe that godparents get the job of raising the kids, should something awful happen to the parents. Fortunately for everyone, those things rarely happened.

Josie was my godmother, but she was also Sicilian, and this was a problem. My grandparents were from Italy, "the old country" where Sicilians were thought of as evil people; they all belonged to the Mafia, and a disgrace to the Italian culture, according to my grandparents. Trying to figure out how Josie could be Sicilian and such a terrific person was really hard for them, especially my grandfather. It was also rumored that Sicilians put raisins into their sauce (gravy) which really made them suspicious. But no matter how much they tried, they couldn't help but love Josie...and so did I. In her defense, she never put a raisen in her sauce.

She was my godmother and my friend. She knew all of my secrets.

My father did not want me playing softball, stickball, basketball or anything that involved sports..He thought girls should be "ladies" and do what "ladies" do. I never found out exactly what that was and so I figured what he didn't know, would make our lives so much easier.

Every summer I played softball for the Police Athletic League, (PAL), a neighborhood organization sponsored by the cops in New

York City. The cops figured if they could keep kids busy they could keep them out of trouble. Sure worked for us.

I learned early in life, when you plan something one way, it's bound to go another...or just tell God you're plans...

One Saturday afternoon, I tried to field a hard hit ground ball. It hit my ungloved hand and I broke my index finger. Immediately my fear of discovery outweighed the pain. Thinking quickly, I set my finger between two ice cream bar sticks, wrapped them tightly and ran to Josie's for help. She agreed to keep my secret as long as I agreed to come by every day so that she could bathe my finger in Epsom salt and re-bandage it. Here we go again with the "hide the hand bit".

After several weeks, the secret was getting really tiresome. I goofed one day, and let down my guard. As I was leaving for school, I reached for my lunch bag with the wrong hand. My mother's reaction was swift but sweet: "I hate when you lie, there isn't anything in the world you can't tell me," she said. The very moment I started to confess, Josie walked in the front door, and sensing what was happening, started to laugh. My mother couldn't resist Josie and began to laugh too.

"You both went through a lot of pain for nothing," my mother said. "Of course I would have covered for you." She said." A little white lie to your father would have been fun."

We all hugged and when I left for school, my hand was outside my pocket, for the first time in weeks.

I continued to play softball until I graduated from high school. My father never did find out about the broken finger nor the many softball games.

Those two gals saved my ass so many times.

She and my mother loved to dance. On Friday nights, after my father left for work, they'd hit the subway for the ride downtown to Roseland, the famed dance palace, where they could dance the night away, always returning before dawn.

Roseland featured the big bands of the day: Benny Goodman, Tommy Dorsey, Guy Lombardo and Artie Shaw.

Josie had a kind of magic about her, a way of turning an ordinary day into something special. She made my mother very happy; they giggled like teenagers, especially on Friday nights. No matter how late they got home, I was always waiting. I loved listening to their stories about the people they met. I always felt so grown up because they trusted me in those moments.

On Friday mornings, before she went off to work, Mom baked either Italian cookies with anisette or chocolate chip cookies and we ate them with joy and drank ice-cold milk when they came back from dancing.

Because of those wonderful memories, Friday night will always be a special night of the week for me.

My father, was an excellent dancer too. He and my Mother danced their dating years, but he would never dance in public after he married unless it was at a family wedding or party. He called it exhibitionism. What would he think of today's social mores? Thank God he never found out about Mom and Josie's weekly excursions to Roseland. So we shared secrets too...softball and dancing.

Several years later, I was terrified to tell my grandfather that I was getting married to someone who was not Italian. I was in love with a handsome young marine pilot who happened to be Irish. Josie suggested I tell grandpa when he was listening to his favorite opera. When I finally got it out, he said, "Thank God he's not Sicilian." He seemed to overlook the fact that Josie was Sicilian. She could do no wrong, and the fact that she was Sicilian was never discussed.

Actually, no one cared what part of Italy she was from because it was Josie.— she was just one of those gems you are lucky to meet once in a lifetime.

CHOCOLATE CHIP COOKIES

This was one of my mother's favorite stories......

"An elderly Italian man lay dying on his bed. While suffering the agonies of impending death, he suddenly smelled the aroma of his favorite anisette sprinkle cookies wafting up the stairs. Gathering his remaining strength, he lifted himself from the bed. Leaning against the wall, he slowly made his way out of the bedroom and with even greater effort, gripping the railing with both hands, crawled downstairs.

With labored breath, he leaned against the door frame, gazing into the kitchen. Were it not for death's agony, he would've thought himself already in heaven. For there, spread out upon waxed paper on the kitchen table, were literally hundreds of his favorite cookies...

Was it heaven? Or was it one final act of heroic love from his devoted Italian wife of sixty years, seeing to it that he left this world a happy man?

Mustering one great final effort, he threw himself toward the table, landing on his knees in a crumpled posture. His parched lips parted, the wondrous taste of the cookie was already in his mouth, seemingly bringing him back to life. The aged and withered hand trembled on its way to a cookie at the edge of the table, when it was suddenly smacked with a spatula by his wife..."Back off!" she said. "They're for the funeral."

CHOCOLATE CHIP
PEANUT BUTTER COOKIES

INGREDIENTS:

1 ¼ cups	all purpose flour
½ tsp.	baking soda
½ tsp.	salt
½ tsp.	ground cinnamon
¾ cup	butter or margarine, soft (1 ½ sticks)
½ cup	granulated sugar
½ cup	packed brown sugar
1 egg	
1 tsp.	vanilla extract
2 cups	Nestle Toll House Semi-Sweet Chocolate Morsels (1 12 oz.. package)
½ cup	coarsely chopped peanuts

DIRECTIONS:

Combine flour, baking soda, salt and cinnamon in small bowl.

Beat butter, granulated sugar, brown sugar and peanut butter in large mixer bowl until creamy.

Beat in egg and vanilla extract. Gradually beat in flour mixture. Stir in chocolate morsels and peanuts.

Drop dough by rounded tablespoons onto ungreased baking sheets. Press down slightly to flatten into 2-inch circles.

Bake in preheated 375º oven for 7 to 10 minutes or until edges are set but centers are soft.

Let stand for 4 minutes. Remove to wire racks to cool completely.

Makes 3 dozen cookies

ROOT BEER FLOATS

Grandmother Rivellino believed that there were no accidents. Everything about a person's life is predestined, she said, and she was the first one to help me understand that I could accomplish anything if I made my mind up to do so. My life's plan was already set in stone according to Grandma. If I wanted it to be. I wish I had seen a bit more of that stone before I made some of my dumber moves.

Growing up in the Bronx was special in the 50's. People talked to and listened to each other. The neighbors would tell stories at night, on the "stoop" during summer, and in our kitchen come winter. The subjects ranged from baseball to cooking to school to who was moving into and out of the neighborhood and about our next trip to Jones Beach on Long Island.

My mother was a good listener and a great cook. With a little garlic, virgin olive oil and some broccoli, she could create a memorable meal and still listen to the babble of the day. My father, who worked nights for the City of New York, left the house at 11pm mumbling stuff like, "Again with these people, what are we running a restaurant?" She'd put food in his mouth, kiss him and shove him out the door. He always left happy, but mumbling.

My mother's food had that effect on everyone except Mr. Rapaport. He owned the local pharmacy and soda fountain at the corner of Barnes Avenue, where we lived. It was the largest soda fountain in The Bronx, with all the shining gadgets spilling out chocolate syrup, seltzer, rootbeer and cherry juice. He was the only person from the neighborhood who never showed up on our "stoop" or in our kitchen.

He didn't seem to like anyone, except me. The other kids were afraid of him. I think we got along because every Saturday, after the movie matinee, I'd use the last of my allowance on one of his huge egg cremes. We'd sit and talk movies for hours. I was only ten when we began our talks, but I loved Bogart, and Betty Davis, Ava Gardner, Rita Haywood, Jimmy Stewart, Cary Grant, Jennifer Jones. There was so much glamour and class up on that big screen then. Maybe that was our connection. Mr. Rapaport was a pharmacist by trade but he was a film critic at heart. He knew more about film than Gene Shalit, Roger Ebert and Rex Reed, today's film critics, all rolled into one.

One Saturday, after we'd decided that *Casablanca* was definitely one of the top ten greatest films of all times, Mr. Rapaport came from behind the soda fountain, sat on the stool next to me and dropped his head in his hands. At first I thought he was sick, but suddenly he blurted out that he missed his wife, who had died on this day, five years before. I had no idea what to say. I started to panic, so I tried to think of what my mother would do. She'd cook something. I got up, went behind the counter and started making a root beer float. Pumping those syrup handles took the fear away immediately. I didn't have a recipe but I'd seen him do this hundreds of times...I pretty much knew it by heart. While I was scooping the ice cream I started thinking about the plot lines for all of my favorite love stories. I started throwing out scenes.

In a flash, it came to me. *Wethering Heights*, with Sir Lawrence Olivier, a stricking handsome man, playing, Heathclifff, Merle Oberon, a beautiful actress playing Cathy, who were not destined to be together while they were alive although they loved each other painfully.

They meet in heaven after they die, and walked the English moors together finding their happiness finally in eternity.

I told Mr. Rapaport that lovers always come together after they die and if that happened in the movies, you know that the odds are great that it will happen in real life too

I wasn't quite sure of this bold statement, but my mother had once told me that whomever you love on Earth, especially your animals, you will meet again in heaven. My mother was a wise woman. If it worked for animals, it must work for people too. So I was making a sad man a little happier with some slight exaggerations.

By the end of the day, we'd each had three root beer floats. Although I didn't know it then, I was beginning to carve out my future. I was on my way to becoming The Godmother.

"VIVE BENE, SPESSO L'AMORE,
DI RISATA MOLTO"
(LIVE WELL, LOVE MUCH
AND LAUGH OFTEN)

AUTHOR UNKNOWN...

ROOT BEER FLOAT

INGREDIENTS:

1 8 oz. per serving of root beer (Dr. Browns is my first Choice, but A&W will do as a good second)

1 quart	Whipping cream
¾ cup	sugar
1 tbs.	vanilla

DIRECTIONS:

Pour the whipping cream, sugar and vanilla into either an electric or a hand crank ice cream maker and turn until it sets.

If you do not own an ice cream maker, Ben and Jerry's French vanilla is a good second choice. Use a pint.

Once the cream has set, scoop out two large servings and put in a tall glass and fill with root beer. Watch the bubbles.

Enjoy!!

SUNDAY DINNER AT GRANDMA'S and SPAGHETTI alla BOLOGNESE

Preparations for Sunday dinner started in the wee hours of Sunday morning. It was usually still dark when my aunts, Elsie and Gemma, arrived at grandma's with families in tow. They needed the time to make the gravy (sauce), which had to simmer for hours and hours.

By the time we got there, grandma already had the meatballs frying in the olive oil and garlic, ready to be put into the sauce pot. Elsie and Gemma were cutting the dough for the spaghetti.

My feet had barely crossed the threshold when Elsie would grab me and announce so everyone could hear, "What a hairdo I got for you, kid!" (I used to think that maybe grandma was blind to what was going on.) With a single motion I was whisked into the bathroom with my mom hurrying in after me, so they could smoke secretly. I was the only kid picked for the tour of duty because I was old enough to keep my mouth shut and I wouldn't squeal no matter what...—"no squealing" was our code in the Bronx. Besides why would I rat out my own Mother?

My cousins, Doreen, Donnalee and Gary, were still little kids and useless for undercover operations. My brother, Nick, who was older than I, was to "grown up for games".

One of the unspoken rules of the day was that no one smoked in front of their mothers or grandmothers.

It was like showing disrespect for these wonderful immigrants who sacrificed so much to be in this "beloved land." Smoking in their presence was somehow unpatriotic and disrespectful and …. It wasn't until years later we found out that it was just pure unhealthy too.

Aunt Gemma didn't smoke so she stayed in the kitchen helping grandma. Maybe our "Nonna" couldn't smell the smoke because of the garlic that was always sautéing on the stove, was my first thought. Years later I figured she was smarter than any of them.

After what seemed like hours in the bathroom, but was probably only ten minutes, the bathroom door opened, and the only thing my mom and aunt had done to my hair was add a few bobby pins and a lot of hair spray. Grandma may not have spoken English very well but she was a smart cannoli…she knew the whole time what was happening in the bathroom, but she enjoyed watching the lengths these ladies went to, to keep their secret. She was a gem—I adored her.

But there was indeed one secret on Sunday's. The family room was at the back of the house—it was a porch, enclosed with removable windows and screens, and on special summer nights, grandpa would take the windows off and we'd sleep out there under the stars. It was grandma's favorite place to sit and knit. It was grandpa's hide-away most of the time.

When we arrived on Sunday mornings, the door was always closed. No one, not even my grandma went in there until after dinner on Sundays. Grandpa said that it was his time with the angels.

Give kids a mystery of sorts and they'll find a way to discover the truth..... and I did just that. One Sunday I decided I wanted to meet his guardian angels. The door wasn't locked, but it sure creaked when I opened it. Grandpa was sitting in his overstuffed chair, his eyes closed. His hand moved as though he was conducting an orchestra. He looked like he was in a trance—he didn't even hear me come in. The voice coming out of the record player was singing in Italian. I couldn't understand a word of it, but my grandpa obviously did. His slender hands swept through the air. He beamed with a kind of mysterious glow. "Grandpa," I whispered as I moved onto the porch, "What is that?" My voice was lost in the music, so I yelled. "GRANDPA!" Startled, his eyes opened and his gaze drifted towards the sound of my voice while his hand still conducted the invisible orchestra. I remember thinking that for that one moment, he didn't seem to be in the room.

"It's Caruso, in La Boheme" he replied. The excitement in his voice told me that what I was listening to was something so unique. I didn't know it then, but it was Enrico Caruso, the great Italian tenor. Not another word was passed between us. I sat at his feet, my head against his bony knees, and listened. I could feel the music inside of my heart. "Dolores, come set the table!" It was my father's voice, but the music wouldn't let go of me. I didn't move. The last note faded with my grandfather's hand resting quietly on my head.

At dinner, I watched my grandpa. He held a green olive in the tips of his fingers and took a bite. From the look on his face I knew he was still in the music. I think he had tears in his eyes. "Pa, how can you like that music? Everyone always dies," my mother said. Everyone dies!! So that's why Caruso sounded so sad. He was singing about death. That drama, that intrigue, was so stimulating to me. Something changed for me that day, but I was too young to figure it out.

When I could understand opera, grandpa told me wonderful stories especially about Caruso. Apparently he was loved by all of his fans and understandably....

In addition to possessing a pure tenor voice, beautiful to hear, to those without admission price to see and hear him at the Metropolitan Opera House in New York, he would pass out complimentary tickets to the Met by the thousands and scrupulously paid for everyone of them.....a bill which often came to over nine thousand dollars per season. ....a very hefty sum in those times. Caruso always used his money to help others..the more he earned, the less it mattered, grandpa said.

SPAGHETTI ALLA BOLOGNESE

INGREDIENTS:

BOLOGNESE

2 tsp.	olive oil
1 tbs.	minced garlic
1 ½ lb.	ground beef
1 28 oz. can	Italian peeled tomatoes, chopped roughly in a cuisinart
1 cup	chicken broth
3/4 cup	chopped basil
2 tbs.	chopped oregano
3	bay leaves
	Godmother salt and some pepper to taste

SPAGHETTI

1 lb.	spaghetti
2 tsp.	kosher salt (my mother's secret)
3 quarts	water
¼ cup	olive oil
	freshly grated parmesan cheese

Add pasta to large pot of boiling water. Do not overcook. Pasta should be al dente "tender but firm to the bite".

Drain and rinse the spaghetti with hot water. Place in bowl and toss with olive oil. Place on a large platter.

SPAGHETTI ALLA BOLOGNESE
(CONTINUED)

DIRECTIONS:

In a medium saucepan, heat the olive oil and add the minced garlic, sautee until golden, then add the ground beef. Sauté until brown. Add the tomato and chicken broth. Lower the heat to a slow simmer,

Then add the chopped basil, oregano, bay leaves, salt and pepper. Simmer on low for 1 - 1 ½ hours. Pour over spaghetti, add parmesan cheese and serve immediately.

"JERRY,
LET'S NOT ASK
FOR THE MOON
WHEN WE ALREADY
HAVE THE STARS."

—BETTE DAVIS
"NOW VOYAGER"

AIDA and EGYPTIAN CHICKEN

I attended my first opera as part of a high school field trip. When I learned we were going to the Metropolitan Opera House in New York City I felt as though someone had given me the keys to a new car. My girlfriends drooled over photos of movie stars, but I always yearned for the opera world since that Sunday with grandpa.

I felt my heart pound as the door to the opera house opened. The ceilings were covered in thick, burgundy cloth and the seats were plush velvet trimmed with regal gold cloth. If you closed your eyes you could almost hear the voices of my grandfather's angels. The walls were covered with photographs of the opera greats: Caruso, GalliCurci, Ponsel.

Heart pounding, hands shaking, I could not imagine what to expect, and, as I sat in my seat, the anticipation of what was about to come left me faint. I couldn't have been any more of a drama queen. My yearnings to work in theater was really showing that day, except no one was around watching my "audition".

A hush fell over the house as the lights dimmed. My eyes were glued to the stage as the overture to Aida began and I waited for the arrival of Zinka Milanov, a very colorful and talented soprano. She walks into the temple of the pyramids singing "Ohime!di Guerra fremere, L'atroce grido io sento, per l'infelice patria, per me, per voi pavento "(Alas, I have heard the frightful war cry sound, I fear for my country, for myself, for you)." Everything I'd heard before but had only been able to imagine came to life. Everything around me dissolved and I was transported into Egypt with the captured princess who fell in love with her captor (the story of Aida).

"There is no hope for my sorrow. Fatal love, fearful love, break my heart and let me die." Her final words pierced my heart.

By the time the curtain fell, my tears had blurred the program in my lap. I was barely a teenager but I'd just experienced passion, love and heartbreak; all in one day.

EGYPTIAN CHICKEN

INGREDIENTS:

2 1/2 to 3 1/2	chickens, cut into 8 pieces each
2 cups	plain yogurt
2 tbs.	lemon juice
2 tbs.	honey
1 tbs.	minced garlic
1 tbs.	tumeric
8	crusted peppercorns
2 cups	cous cous
1 3/4 cups	boiling chicken broth
1/2 tsp.	cinnamon
1/2 cup	toasted slivered almonds
1/2 cup	currants

DIRECTIONS:

Rinse the chicken in cold water; drain and pat dry.

In a medium bowl, whisk together yogurt, lemon juice, honey, garlic, turmeric and peppercorns. Pour over chicken and marinate in refrigerator for 1 hour.

Heat oven to 375⁰.

Place marinated chicken on a roasting pan. Cook uncovered at 375⁰ for 45 minutes. Place cous cous in a medium bowl. Stir in cinnamon, olive oil and currants. Pour boiling chicken broth over chicken, cover with plastic wrap and let stand for 20 minutes. Uncover, flake with a fork, place on a warm platter and top with toasted slivered almonds.

Place Egyptian chicken in the center of a platter, and add the cous cous around the chicken.

Serve with heated flat bread and yogurt.

Serves 8

IL VALORE DEL SORRISO
NON COSTA NIENTE MA
DA MOLTO.

THE VALUE OF A SMILE
COSTS NOTHING AND
GIVES A LOT.

—HARRY CHIAMULERA
FROM THE BRONX

MARIA CALLAS and ROAST CHICKEN

There is no way that you have gotten this far without realizing that I really do believe in angels, most of the time.

I used to think they were only in heaven; loved ones who had passed on to the great "white way" and who come back every so often to make sure you're not screwing up too badly. I never thought I had a personal one here on Earth. I found one of my first guardian angel in the strangest place.

I was working in the personnel department at the Commodore Hotel, which was then attached to the famous Grand Central Station in New York City. My guardian angel appeared on the front page of the Daily News one morning. The photo was a scathing one of Maria Callas, the controversial soprano who was screaming at a some guy trying to serve her a subpoena after her performance at the Chicago Lyric Opera House in Chicago, Illinois. Not an attractive image, certainly not one you'd think of as an angel.

My boss, an extraordinarily bright and compulsive guy,was one of the most frustrating people I've ever worked for before or since.

Francis Herbert Hoover was his name (he was named after the thirty-first president of the United States. That will give you some idea of this guys's pedigree) and opera was his game. He had been yapping at me for months about this woman. You'd have though she walked in Mother Teresa's shoes. He shoved the newspaper in my face., "This is the wonderful Maria Callas, the greatest soprano of the century!", he said. "Yeah, yeah, yeah", I replied. "She doesn't look so great in that photo." The look on his face told me that he thought I was one of the all-time biggest jerks and totally ignorant too.

He was somewhat of a snob...sweet but a snob so I was really playing into his already prejudiced idea of my intellectual capacities.

When I arrived at work the following morning, I found two tickets to the opera Tosca on my desk. Herb was tired of my cynicism, the note said, and he wanted me to see for myself what 'greatest' really was. My pal, Marie Riccardi, who shared the every day hilarious moments of working in the personnel department of this large hotel said, "he probably has had too much sun again." (a year before Herb was told by some 'genius' physician to stay out of the sun for three years and his illness which was never explained completely to him, would go away.) That "prescription" was always good for many laughs.

I never turn down a challenge or free tickets to the opera so I prepared myself for Maria. (I thought)

The following week, Dian, my best friend and I walked into the Metropolitan Opera House for only my second visit. I was hyperventilating. As we entered the lobby, we were surrounded by the grandeur of the interior with its fluted and gilded pillars. The "old Met" was such a magnificent building— years of wear and tear didn't distract from its commanding appearance*. I thought to myself that I hadn't seen the chandeliers before, had they been there when I saw Aida?

The ushers were dressed in black tie with tails. I felt as though I was a guest at a Victorian era party. Women were dressed in flowing gowns, men in dark suits and some in tuxedos yet. ...definitely a black tie affair. How exciting. Of course, those "tuxedos" were sitting in the Orchestra section; we had dress circle seats, which were not so shabby either.

(*The elegant new Metropolitan is located at Lincoln Center 40 blocks away.)

Located on the second floor tier, the seats gave a full view of the stage, and the movement of the audience entering their seats...good seats for the price.

The first time I came to the Met, I was dressed in my best high school clothes. This day, I actually looked like a lady, in a rather sophisticated blue silk dress, wearing high heels. Although I dislike wearing make-up, Dian, had insisted that make-up was a must especially for this special evening. I will admit that a little powder and rouge went a long way on me that night. I actually looked pretty good.

The heart starts pounding again, the palms perspiring as the overture began and when the curtain rose, before us was a replica of the interior of the Church of Sant'Andrea della Valle in Rome in 1800. (The first scene in the opera TOSCA)

From the moment I heard Maria's' voice off stage singing, "Mario, Mario, Mario," I was hooked.

She moved on stage like a force determined to be heard as she pleaded with her lover.

When the opera ended, I couldn't move. This woman made the music tragic, but hauntingly beautiful. I felt as though Tosca was someone I knew in another lifetime, which is remarkable, since I'm talking about other worlds that I don't normally believe exist (except when something extraordinary occurs, of course). She did so much more than just sing the role.

She made me feel as though I was in nineteenth century Rome, walking the cobbled stone streets, afraid that the villain Baron Scarpia, "the despotic and perfidious chief of the Roman police" was plotting to get me too.

She was Tosca, passionately in love with Mario Cavaradossi, who would tragically die before the evening ends. Nothing was make-believe that night, It felt as though I held my breath for hours. I didn't of course...my chest just felt that way.. I felt the cold walls of Castel Sant'Angelo, where Mario was to be executed. No wonder grandpa cried every time he heard Caruso. I finally realized that it was never the opera alone for him, it was Caruso and the drama. After that night, it would always be Callas for me, and of course, the drama too.

You could have a million bucks and tell yourself your happy, but if you haven't found that special thing inside of you that motivates you to find your center, aura or whatever the hell you call it, then you better keep trying because you'll never find the true wealth of life without it. I had found my Angel.

The ride home on the subway that night, was very difficult. Herb kept repeating, "I told you so." I was trying to savor the evening and he was gloating. It was understandable, but he was relentless and so annoying...wouldn't stop repeating, "I told you so".

He never knew how close he came to being pushed onto the tracks. He would have looked awful with all the underbelly of the subway system on him... But he would have deserved it.

I had an epiphany that night, the kind that makes you feel like your head is being slammed in by a two-by-four; the one where you hear voices, and you hope you can call it 'intuition.' The voices told me that "whatever you do, do it right."

To do it right, I sure went every which way.

When I graduated from Evander, a friend of my mother's got me a job which might have had a future, but the job was so boring. To amuse myself, I would throw metal paper clips into the electric typewriters from across the room. This creates huge sparks if you hit the typewriter at the right spot. It was like the Fourth of July everyday. I was hoping this job would turn into a career in journalism but the American Newspaper Publishers Association had no sense of humor.

I was a store detective at Lord & Taylors, the very up scale, expensive store on Fifth Avenue in New York, during my college days. I was good at it too. My strong intuition works well with shoplifters especially.

I caught my quota of ten shoplifters every month and even caught someone I graduated with from Evander. (I let her go, because she had a very sad story)

Because I charged all of my Lord & Taylor clothing purchases to my salary, I was the best dressed but most financially destitute detective. When I left to get married, I owed Lord & Taylors a fortune.

After my hospital career, I ran a gold and diamond company. My family and friends were bedecked in jewels (I am not the jewel type) I was looking, and looking, and then I found it. I wanted to be Callas. Not the soprano, but the character. I wanted to inhale and love whatever I was doing like Callas did. She didn't just stand on stage and sing. She embodied the heart and soul of her operatic characters. She went beyond her amazing voice and risked it all to give both her audience and herself the experience of living the part.

I became obsessed. The very next day, I started to save money, working overtime at the hotel whenever I could.

I even went so far as to work as a babysitter for the neighbors, even though I had always disliked doing it: dealing with screaming and snot-nosed kids, even if their parents sweetened the pot and left me homemade cannolis. It was not my idea of a fun evening. But I needed the money so I could buy everything Callas ever recorded. And through the years, I succeeded... even the bootlegged stuff.

We (Dian, Alan, Herb and I) found the bootlegged recordings (recorded from the prompters box below the stage during the live performance and sold on the 'black market'), in Brooklyn, a borough I had never been to before or since. Some guy, living in a dark, scary house with heavy drapes acted as though he was selling us cocaine. He spoke in whispers. We felt as though the cops were waiting around the block to 'bust' us. We paid him ten bucks per album and hit the highway before he put the money in his pocket.

Luckily, my three friends are equally obsessed. We have been dear friends and Callas devotees for more than forty years..from that very first Tosca when we became inseparable. I have since moved to Malibu and Herbert moved to San Francisco. Dian and Alan have remained in New York.

We ate, slept and drank Callas, during our New York days. At least twice a month, we'd have dinners with Herb and Alan at their spacious apartment on Seventy-second Street.. No one had any money. Dian made a mean pasta primavera and I roasted chicken from my mother's favorite Sunday dish recipe.

How can you beat it? The juices spilling all over you as you bite into the crispy and juicy skin of this delicious chicken, and the pan-roasted potatoes melting in your mouth? The boys bought cheap wine, but the only thing we cared about was Callas and our passion to talk about and listen to her music. We were social outcasts—no one wanted to spend a moment with the four of us together. To the rest of world, we were bores.

One very hot and muggy summer New York night, the opera Tosca was blaring through the apartment. The french doors were open in the hope of getting a breath of air. The music traveled down Seventy-second Street and across the park. And at the moment Maria was singing her celebrated aria "Vissi d'arte, her poignant appeal against the injustice of fortune that has thus rewarded a life that has been dedicated to art and music, to piety and acts of human kindness."

Herb interrupted our moment. "You know I truly love this woman, even if she doesn't hit the high 'C' every time." We pelted him with whatever we could get our hands on—uncooked carrots, potatoes and onions. Who cared if she missed a high 'C' (and she certainly wasn't going to miss it now on this recording), so why are you disturbing our moment? No one noticed when I put too much garlic in the roasted chicken, did they? We never wanted to hear any criticism of Maria, even if it came with love and good-intentions. Callas was more than just her voice, perfect or not. Callas was royalty, she was untouchable. She was our guardian angel. Nothing could make us happier at that moment, except if she had walked through the french doors.

WOULD YOU BELIEVE?

For the past forty-five Easter Sundays, Alan telephones me and plays Regina Coeli (the Easter Hymn) from the extremely emotional opera, Cavalleria Rusticana where Maria Callas' voice soars passionately over the entire chorus. Alan has never missed an Easter, no matter where he has travelled; London, Paris, Milan, Saigon, Singapore, St. Petersburg. The mystery is how he has managed to find a record player of any kind in so many cities under some of the strangest circumstances.

HONEY BAKED CHICKEN &
PAN ROASTED POTATOES

INGREDIENTS:

THE CHICKEN

2 tbs.	garlic
3 sprigs	rosemary
¼ - ½ cup	honey
1 cup	soy sauce
10 quartered	pieces of chicken

THE POTATOES

6 medium	red rose potatoes, cut in fourths
1/4 cup	olive oil
1 tbs.	Dijon mustard
1 tsp.	garlic, chopped fine
2 tsp.	rosemary, fresh leaves, chopped fine
1/4 tsp.	coarse salt and pepper

DIRECTIONS:

THE CHICKEN

Preheat oven to 375°.

In a 9x13 pan, pour the soy sauce, drizzle in the honey, add the garlic and fresh rosemary leaves; stir. Place the quartered chicken pieces skin-down in the baking pan, and place in 375° oven for 30 minutes. Turn chicken pieces over so skin side is up, place back in oven for 30 minutes.

Remove chicken from baking pan to serving dish, reserve sauce in bottom of pan, skim off any extra grease. Serve with chicken.

4 SERVINGS

HONEY BAKED CHICKEN & PAN ROASTED POTATOES
(CONTINUED)

<u>THE POTATOES</u>:

Preheat oven to 400º.

Wash red rose potatoes, pat dry, and cut oblong into quarters.

In a medium mixing bowl, add the olive oil, Dijon mustard, chopped garlic and rosemary, salt and pepper, and mix well. Add the oblong quarters of potatoes, tossing until well-coated.

Place the potato quarters on an oiled baking sheet, place in 400º oven for 20 minutes. Turn potato pieces over and continue baking for another 20 minutes. Remove from oven and serve immediately.

4 SERVINGS

LA TRAVIATA, BALLOONS AND PARTY FAVORS

I was never one to miss an opportunity, especially if it was starring me in the face.

Maria Callas was singing La Traviata at the Metropolitan Opera House on the night of Dian's twenty-first birthday. Nothing was going to stop me from getting us there. Realizing we couldn't scrape up enough money to buy even one ticket, I knew I had to do some creative financing. I took out a loan from Chemical Corn Exchange Bank for forty-five dollars to be repaid in three months: fifteen dollars a month plus interest. My first bank loan ever. Certainly not my last.

Boy, have we seen the last of those days—the tickets were only nine dollars each, and we were sitting in my favorite spot, dress circle.

The evening began with dinner at the famed New York Plaza Hotel's Edwardian Room, compliments of Herb and Alan. Herb was now the personnel director at the Plaza and arranged a sumptuous birthday dinner.

Having any meal at The Edwardian Room in the famed Plaza Hotel had always been a dream for Dian. For a girl from the Bronx, she had great taste. For the rest of us, it was as luxurious as flying the Concorde to Paris for a night.

The setting was perfect. I have no clue what we ate... except for the dessert. It was a pastiere. I can still taste the delectable mix of vanilla and cream with fresh lemon peel.

Dian's cousin, Yola, a very talented florist, created a beautiful bouquet of camellias (the flower favored by the heroine in La

Traviata). We were giddy with our plans to rush the stage to throw the flowers at Maria's feet.

It was a crushing blow when we walked into the opera house and discovered that signs posted all over the lobby warned against that very thing: "Anyone throwing flowers on stage would be ejected from the theater and possibly prosecuted for a misdemeanor" Management feared a Renata Tibaldi and Maria Callas fan club riot. What they considered a riot in those days was laughable. Personally, I thought it was a great public relations scheme to heighten interest and sell more tickets. The most violence we'd ever seen was someone yelling at each other.... Remember, this was the 50's—this was the Metropolitan Opera House.......violence was peaceful, especially among classical opera lovers. But with the flowers tucked under my dress, I had a problem. I had to do some fast thinking.

The performance was another masterpiece of interpretation by Callas. Even our own personal "critic" Herb thought so.

Before the curtain came down, I ran down the stairs with the bouquet hidden under my dress (as strange as it sounds now, I wore dresses once).... and pushed my way to the front of the stage. A tall, gangly teenage boy jammed up against me clapping and crying at the same time. The audience was yelling out Maria's name, and before I knew what was happening, I turned to the young man and said, "I'll pay you five bucks if you throw these flowers up there." Without responding, he grabbed the five dollar bill and threw the bouquet. "Oh my God, it landed at her feet!" I said. I know she heard me, because she looked at me, smiled, and picked up the bouquet. She hugged the flowers for the next ten curtain calls. A bully of a guard quickly grabbed the kid and took him outside. He was released later and was five dollars richer for the thrill of it all.

Nothing could stop me now—I had to find a way to get backstage. I told my friends, "We're going back...follow me and keep your mouths shut."

"You're certifiable!" Herb, such a worrier, said.

"We'll be arrested for sure," Dian chimed in.

"Oh, my God, I'll be deported!" Alan, a British subject said. Now tell me, do you know of any Brit who has ever been deported?

"I know what I'm doing so just do what I do and act like you belong!" I was a bulldog that night more so than ever before. Nothing was going to stop me, I had to get backstage and see Maria.

My friends behaved like well-trained puppies. I approached the stage door with an air of familiarity and the guard didn't even question us. He opened the door and moved aside to let us pass, and at the same time, he held the throngs of fans from pushing backstage.

We were entering the backstage of the Metropolitan Opera House, where in one of those small dressing rooms, the great Maria Callas was removing her make-up. I was shaking with excitement. This wasn't real.

Grandma said, "You can't stop destiny. You can get in her way, but you can't stop her." We walked slowly down the hall of this great theater to avoid any suspicion that maybe we didn't belong there. We hugged the walls and each other trying to appear 'normal'. People were hugging all over the place congratulating friends and family who had performed on this special night.

The walls were filled with more pictures of the great opera singers of the past in roles that had made them famous: Enrico Caruso in *I Pagliacci*, Lilly Pons in *Lakme*, and Jussi Bjorling in *Rigoletto*.

Suddenly, we were at her dressing room. Her name was on the door....lettered in a black tipped pen.... "good penmanship," I remarked, for lack of knowing what else to say. The door was ajar. My friends were following so closely they fell into me when I suddenly stopped and we all practically fell into the room. Not a very glamorous entrance. We brushed ourselves off and stood in front of Maria Callas. Face to face, we were starring at Maria Callas. My throat was dry. I couldn't say a word. I thought she'd throw us out, but then she laughed. A huge, throaty laugh. She recognized me. She was sipping orange soda from the largest bottle I'd ever seen, when the words just fell out of my mouth, "Hi, Maria. I'm Dolores Walsh and these are my friends. We came to tell you how wonderful you are, and we threw those camellias to you on stage." (the "we" was a bit of an exaggeration)

Smiling she offered us a drink from her orange bottle. We shook our heads, "No" although, I would've sold Herb for a swig of that orange soda pop.

The next morning a photo of Maria holding our flowers was plastered on the front page of every New York newspaper. The caption read *"TOASTING HER WITH CHEERS...Holding a bouquet, thrown to her from her fans, Maria Callas accepts the plaudits of audience at the Metropolitan after her first appearance there as Violetta in "La Traviata". Maria got rave notices to follow her Roman blowup".*

Toasting Her With Cheers

Holding a bouquet, Maria Callas accepts the plaudits of audience at the Met after her first appearance there as Violetta in "La Traviata." Maria got rave notices to follow her Roman blowup.

Our bouguet of 'Camellia's' the kid threw Maria that night. The only one she received on stage.

MARIA CALLAS and RISOTTO ALLA PILOTA

When we left Maria that night, she asked me to call her at 11:30 the following morning, putting her phone number into my hand. I was so cool about it I never looked at the paper until I was on the street. I ran out of the Met because I was afraid she would have heard my knees shaking.

Of course I didn't sleep that night. I was too wound up and besides I was afraid I'd miss my appointed time to call.

At 6am, I started checking my watch every fifteen minutes for the next five and a half hours. As 11:30 approached, I started thinking, "Well, maybe it's too early for her to be up." The next thing I knew I was holding the receiver, "Hi, is Maria available? It's Dolores Walsh calling." Where did that courage come from? I was calling the greatest opera singer of our century like she was my best friend.

From the moment she picked up the phone, it was indeed like talking to an old friend. "Oh dear Dolores, I hope you are well." And then, "Too many lawyers, agents, impresarios, too many demands. I'm suffocating, they call me a diva but all I want to do is sing. I'm not a diva." She said all of this without taking a breath.

I listened carefully and lovingly and didn't have a solid thought in my head, except that I was thrilled, for the moment, to be somewhat of a confidant to this extraordinary woman. I was sure then that she probably did this with anyone who she liked and who called her at these low moments. Celebrity can be a lonely state. I know better now. There were many talks through the years. Although I'll never share the details of any of our conversations, I can say that she often said "You must love what you do, whatever that is."

November 22, Maria Callas was performing at Constitution Hall in Washington, D.C. We slept at the "Y"—The Young Women's Christian Association and it cost us $1.18 per night....this we could afford, but we were strapped for money. We begged, borrowed, and stopped just short of stealing to get what ended up being the worst seats in the auditorium. But a last-minute walk across the Washington Mall was a stroke of good fortune. We found a bag full of coins, (probably twelve bucks) and after dutifully looking for a possible owner, we ran quickly for fear of actually finding that person. We were thrilled with the dinner we ate, (hamburgers and fries) but when we arrived at the Hall, I was so frustrated when I saw the seats—they were so far up in the balcony that with my hay fever, I would have needed oxygen.

I hadn't come all this way and sacrificed hot meals not to be able to see her, and in the interest of my sanity and health, I had to think of something quickly.

There is a fine line between insanity and obsession. My friends were convinced that I was insane. I knew that I was obsessed. Semantics!!!!!

Sometimes, I concluded denial is such a comfortable state. Off I went to the stage door. With three loud, determined knocks, a woman answered. Obviously, she was not overjoyed to see me—the scowl on her face would have terrified most people, but the bulldog in me was determined to get better seats. "Please tell Madam Callas that Dolores Walsh is here," I said. She slammed the door in my face. I waited. Something told me that she'd be back. An eternity passed.

Finally the door opened and a hand extended a ticket with a note. The scowling lady never showed her face again. I grabbed the ticket and the note and ran back to the auditorium. I read the note as I stopped to get my breath: "Come backstage later. Maria." I gave the ticket to an usher who escorted me down to the center aisle orchestra. As we walked to the front of the auditorium, I could hear my friends utter, "Son of a xoxo" The words seemed to float down from the balcony. They were very clear and precise.

"Son of a xoxo"

My seat was in the third row, to the left of the stage, next to her father, a kind looking gentleman who seemed overwhelmed by the occasion. I nodded to him as I sat down. He smiled and returned the greeting. I easily recognized him because I had seen him in many newspaper articles alongside Maria.

The moment Maria stepped out onto the stage and started to sing, he seemed stunned. After the first aria and the thunderous applause, he turned to me and whispered, "Is she doing good?" I couldn't believe he was asking me if his daughter, Maria Callas, the most amazing opera singer in the world, was doing good. "Oh, yes sir," I said emphatically. "She is doing VERY good."

After the concert we talked for a few minutes. He had attended very few of her performances because he worked as a pharmacist in New York City and couldn't take the time off. He had to come to Washington, although he felt somewhat guilty for leaving his job. But

Maria had requested him and he wanted to be there for her. He was such a proud father that night.

I didn't think things could get any better for me. But they did. The curtain fell to thunderous applause and a standing ovation. Her father wept. Moments later we were backstage. We were the receiving line…Alan, Dian, Dolores, Maria, Menenghini, her husband and her father. We were the receiving line greeting celebrities; Senators, Congressmen, news media, friends. This was certainly better than anything Hollywood could dream up.

A reporter moved himself behind us and asked, "What connection do you all have to Maria?" What could I tell this guy? So I pretended to be too busy meeting my admirers to hear. He moved over to Alan, who satisfied him with a simple, "We're old friends."

That experience of meeting so many celebrities at one time really conditioned me for my future life in Malibu. I have never been in awe of any celebrity and maybe that's because that particular evening, when I tasted it, I was seeing what it would be like on the other side. It's tough to stand there and be the focus for a couple of hours. To be starred down, to be pushed and shoved and subjected to so many questions.

We were getting this treatment because the press had no clue who we were and wanted to know desperately what the hell we were doing on a receiving line with the great diva, Maria Meneghini Callas.

Before I finish this story, let me tell you how we do it today in Malibu.

Malibuites have a great deal of respect for the celebrities and give them lots of private space along with honoring and respecting their right to live normal lives. ….. That doesn't mean if I'd run into

into Brad Pitt, my knees wouldn't go to mush...but I would never approach him unless he made the first move and if —Brad Pitt made the first move, you could bet your life he would stir some juices that haven't been stirred in years in this old broad. I think he's adorable and my intuition, tells me a nice guy too. But then again I think that Ed Harris, Pierce Brosnan, Robert Redford, Paul Newman are all nice guys.

When the mass of people backstage started to leave, we made a move toward the door too. But Maria asked us if we'd like to join her for supper back at her hotel. We looked at each other, a trifle startled, as I said quickly, "Oh that would be nice Madam Callas, if, of course you're not too tired." This was a dream, and we would be waking soon, I thought. Where did those words come from? "Oh, that would be nice"

When we arrived at the hotel, the table was set with fine china, crystal and sterling silver.

I have never seen this type of personal service in any hotel I've ever been to in this country or abroad. But I have never been in another hotel with the likes of MARIA CALLAS.

A chef-like person came out of the kitchen and asked how we liked our eggs cooked! Who could eat? I don't remember what I responded.

Maria settled in a huge, comfortable looking chair in the living room and we melted into down cushioned couches that were scattered around the room. Another waiter passed coffees and waters, and Maria began immediately to tell us the story of risotto alla pilota:

"Antonio Ghiringhelli, director of La Scala, and Tullio Serafin, my dear friend and conductor, hated each other. Ghiringhelli wouldn't let me sing Norma, and no one could every figure out why not. Then, late in 1949, I had just finished performing in Rome, Naples, Florence and Genoa. One night in Milan, Serafin, my husband Batista and I decided to go to Biffi Scala, the celebrated restaurant near the opera house. Ghiringhelli was there too.

Ordinarily, Serafin would have ignored Ghiringhelli but this night, he decided to be friendly. He was thinking that with me right there, perhaps a conversation might lead to the possibility for me to sing Norma at La Scala. We all knew that Ghiringhelli had experienced a world shortage of Normas. He had a disaster miscasting the role the year before. But he was bitter and stubborn.

"'To do Norma is not as difficult as you think,' Ghiringhelli told Serafin as I sat by, quietly miserable. "As a matter of fact, I intend to present one that will make history!" "Ah, yes? And how do you propose to do that?" Serafin responded. Ghiringhelli had no Normas in the works and all four of us knew it. He blustered and repeated himself, but before he could retreat, Serafin said, "I am from Rottanove. Italy. We have a famous rice dish in our area. Risotto alla pilota. Do you know what you need to make risotto alla pilota? The rice!"

"I was the rice Serafin was referring to. It took two long years for Ghiringhelli to let me do Norma but it became Milan's greatest operatic presentation and my most famous and acclaimed role!"

I didn't know it then, but that would be the last time I would see Maria for quite a while. Once again, her words had pierced my soul. I left that night knowing that I had to do something special. I had to find that talent within me that would leave an imprint on someone else. I needed to find my reason for being on Earth. How much more dramatic could I be??? Suppose I had no talents? Well, I could always become a politician.

(Maria Callas left a lasting legacy and was truly a legend. I was priviledged to be her friend.)

RISOTTO ALLA PILOTA

INGREDIENTS:

5 cups	canned low-salt chicken broth
4 tbs.	(½ stick) butter
1 cup	finely chopped onion
1 ½ cups	arborio rice
1 cup	grated parmesan cheese
2 tbs.	chopped fresh Italian parsley
2 cups	shaved parmesan cheese

DIRECTIONS:

Bring broth to a boil in medium saucespan. Reduce heat to low and cover the saucepan. Melt 2 tablespoons butter in a heavy medium saucepan over medium-low heat. Add onions; sautee with a little butter until very tender but do not brown (about 15 minutes).

Add rice and stir 1 minute.

Add 1 cup warm broth.

Boil gently until broth is absorbed, stirring frequently.

Add another cup of broth; stir until broth is absorbed.

Add remaining 3 cups broth, ½ cup at a time, allowing broth to be absorbed before adding more. Stir frequently until rice is tender and mixture is creamy (about 25 minutes.)

Stir in 2 tablespoons butter and 1 cup grated cheese. Season with salt and pepper.

Transfer to bowl. Sprinkle with parsley and shaved parmesan.

Serves 4 as a first course

6 as a side dish

MARIA and GREEK MEATBALLS

The bells of St. Patrick's Day chimed. It was midnight in New York. Maria was aboard the Christina, Onnasis's yacht, in the middle of the Mediterranean. We talked many times in the middle of the night when she was away. She said that she was eating Greek meatballs and drinking Ouzo. I was chopping oregano and basil for a Bolognese sauce.

"When you feel passionate about something, anything, like how I feel about my music and the way it should be performed, don't settle for less..." Here we go again. She was like a broken record about not settling for less. I don't know what she thought I was capable of doing, but I listened and was thrilled to be having any conversation with her.

I held the receiver so tight to my head that my ear started to get hot and painful but I didn't want to miss a word. I was waiting breathlessly for what was next to come.

Hummmmmmmm!!! The connection went dead. Damn! I tried for hours to get her back on the phone but all circuits were busy.

But I did get the recipe for her Greek meatballs...

GREEK MEATBALLS

INGREDIENTS:

1 slice	Italian bread, ½ inch cubes
¼ cup	milk
1 lb.	ground lamb
1 tsp.	garlic, minced
2 tbs.	scallion, minced
1/3 cup	fresh mint, minced
1/4 cup	feta cheese, crumbled
1/4 tsp.	black pepper
3 tbs.	olive oil, heated
¼ tsp.	cinnamon
28 oz.	Italian tomatoes, canned, crushed
2 tbs.	fresh mint, chopped
1 large pinch	red pepper flakes
3 oz.	feta cheese, crumbled
1	egg
	Godmother salt to taste

DIRECTIONS:

Preheat oven to 375⁰.

In a small bowl, mix milk and bread and soak for a few minutes.

In a medium bowl, mix together the milk-soaked bread, ground lamb, garlic, scallions, black pepper and cinnamon. Let rest for 15 minutes.

Form two inch round meatballs and place on ungreased cookie sheet. Place meatballs in oven at 375⁰, then cook 15-20 minutes until done.

While meatballs are cooking, make the tomato feta sauce.

GREEK MEATBALLS
(CONTINUED)

Pour the olive oil into a large sauce pan and add the minced garlic, sauté until golden.

Add the can of crushed Italian tomatoes, salt and pepper to taste. Simmer for 30 minutes, add the cooked meatballs. Simmer for one hour on low. Add the minced mint, crumbled feta cheese and crushed red peppers.

Makes 4 servings

OPERA IS LIFE WITH MUSIC...
LIFE IS OPERA WITHOUT MUSIC...

MARIA CALLAS

BANANA SPLITS

After school every day, we gathered at the The Evander Sweet Shoppe, our local hangout. We all looked alike because we wore the same clothes; the school sweater, black and orange with a big "E" if you earned it for a sport which most of us did; wool skirts and most importantly, white buck shoes, especially in summer.. A bag of powder was included when you bought your white bucks... very important ...and key item. White bucks had to be clean and sparkling white. However the "cool ones", never cleaned their shoes if someone was looking. But there is always someone who doesn't care if he cleans his bucks in front of anyone....and we had one of those....loved to talk about himself, even if no one was listening.

And talk he did, actually bragging; about his grades, his good looks, his white buck shoes... on and on and on.

He was the first person I ever knew, and certainly not the last, who had an answer for everything.

We got enough answers from our teachers and parents and adults in general, we didn't want to hear any more especially from another kid. One of his favorite subjects was his endless talk about money and Hollywood. ..."Someday he'd be rich and we'd be sooooooooo oooooooooooenvious...."

We were juniors in high school and we were SO not interested in success, money, or some place called Hollywood. That's where movie stars lived; why would anyone want to live there? No snow, no subways, no Yankee Stadium, no Broadway...Give us a break.... Some one should have unplugged him. Our crowd on the other hand, was all about banana splits and Saturday night dates.

Fast forward twenty years. I am visiting one of my dearest friend, Susie Orma, also known as "Blaks", who was an accountant at Burbank Studios, in Los Angeles. As I pulled into the studio parking lot, I noticed a painted name on one of the reserved parking spaces which was the same as Mr. "Know It All." Could it be the same guy? Sure was. He was the executive producer of the most popular television program in the history of television. A marvelous show, and Valerie's all time favorite. Susie said he was not the most-liked guy on the lot. No surprise to me. He achieved his life's ambition.

Grandma said, "You don't know a thing unless you're under the bed." In this case, I never wanted to be anywhere near this guy's bed, but I'm happy for him. Who knows how he did it! Maybe he threw away the 'white bucks' and enjoys life now. He sure made his dream come true.

In our senior year, the theme for our yearbook was FOOD. We lived in a ethnic neighborhood so why wouldn't it be food?

Our parents and grandparents were proud to set a table with bowls of warm delicious pastas, roast chicken, grilled fish and plenty of vegetables and fresh fruit foods for their families every night. To them, this was a mark of success. Eating is a biological occurrence, but it is also a cultural phenomenon. Our senior class wanted to honor this tradition, and made the theme of the class yearbook "glorious food".

The senior class big-shots were called Senior Chefs. Our four years were divided into courses: Freshman year was the salad course; Sophomore, the soup; Junior year was the fruit; Senior year, the entrée. Graduation was naturally dessert. Because cheese is known for its sharp, sometimes spicy, pungent flavor, the twenty-three leaders of the senior class were called "The Big Cheeses." They ran the senior year, and we tried all kinds of recipes; Recipes for going to college, Recipe for a Noisy Lunchroom, Recipe for Failing a Regent (you couldn't graduate without passing New York State Regent Exams), Recipe for Indigestion, Recipe for a Late Pass.

I was slowly but surely indoctrinated with food in every part of my life. Those were the beginning seeds for the 'growing" of what turned out to be the Godmother of Malibu.

I loved food and I love writing. Now where????

My Grandma and Mom were the most talented and creative cooks I knew, but they never made a penny doing it. I was single and needed to pay the rent. Writing seemed like the only logical solution. I wasn't skilled enough to go work for a restaurant. My brother Nick was a very talented and successful chef. He worked for some of the finest hotels and restaurants in New York and Los Angeles. Let me repeat he had real talent.

Even with my 'charming ways' I couldn't pull that one off....

I decided to try the writing thing first. I just had to figure out what it was that I wanted to write, and how I could earn a living doing it. I love books, besides food and opera; they are another passion of mine that never seems to get satisfied. What was I thinking?

It's a good thing I found other work to support my life styles. I would have starved to death for good reasons, if I had tried to earn a dime writing. Hello!!! You need to have extraordinary talent.

61

I cherish the work of Virginia Wolfe who although beat to a strange drummer boy was vibrant and brilliant in her writings; or Edith Wharton whose fine sense of language was such a God-given talent. I enjoy the books of Anne Lamott because of her ruthless honesty and ability to express herself spiritually with so much humor. What was I thinking.

New York common sense prevailed, and I abandoned the writing crave and took the other road; the one to the Godmother where I discovered my own fine, creative and extraordinary abilities to put it all together.

This cookbook, which is as far from a work of literature as is the instructions to assembling a "Teeter tot" has taken almost ten years to finish. It probably would have been done long ago had I had lots of leisure time, a head full of free flowing thoughts and words and a TRUST FUND.

The cold reality is that it did take years, it isn't a work of genius but it's what the Godmother is all about... so enjoy!!!!!!

BANANA SPLITS

INGREDIENTS:

½ cup	heavy cream
½ vanilla bean	split and scraped of seeds
4 bananas	peeled and split lengthwise
4 scoops (about ½ pint)	coffee ice cream
4 scoops	chocolate ice cream
4 scoops	hazelnut ice cream
½ cup	chocolate syrup
½ cup	caramel sauce
handful of walnuts	
Fresh or brandied cherries	

DIRECTIONS:

In a medium bowl, whip cream and vanilla bean seeds until soft peaks form. Place 2 banana halves in each of four dishes. Top with one scoop each of coffee, chocolate and hazelnut ice cream. Drizzle with chocolate syrup and caramel sauce. Top with whipped cream, walnuts and cherries; serve.

Serves 4

4 scoops = ½ pint approximately

part two

SWIMMING WITH THE FISHES

One rainy morning in New York, I decided to comb the classified section of the Sunday papers. I needed a big change in my life. I figured there must be a job lurking somewhere between the ads for auto mechanics and topless waitresses.

I'd had two cups of coffee before I found it hidden between personal trainers and pizza delivery. "Personnel director for prestigious hospital in Los Angeles needed." A hospital in Los Angeles! Like the movies..."Heartbreak filled with love and passion"...I could feel a story about to happen. So I went to California with stars in my eyes. I was looking for the things I saw on the BIG SCREEN to happen, this was the magic kingdom. Anything was possible. Maybe I'd find something to write about.

I spent the better part of my childhood at the movies. The lessons I learned were priceless. How to kiss from Cary Grant, how to smoke from Humphrey Bogart (along with my aunts and my mom). I loved the glamorous beauties like Lana Turner, Rita Hayworth, Marilyn Monroe, and the my personal favorite, Ava Gardner.

My God, they were incredibly gorgeous women with such classic style who lit up the screen. It didn't matter whether or not they could act...who cared! Sometimes the thought crossed my mind that maybe I should become an actress. I immediately rejected that thought because looking at these women, it was obvious that being gorgeous and having a powerful sexual allure were sort of prerequisites. I didn't have any of that stuff. I barely wanted to wash my face in those days.

I could work behind the scenes and try directing. What a dreamer I was. I thought this might be an easier job that didn't require much skill, just a big mouth... and that I had. I practically directed everyone I ever knew. (I want to take this opportunity to apologize to all of my director friends for my ignorance... I've learned that there is no harder job in the 'biz' than THE DIRECTOR.) No matter what I might direct, however, it wasn't going to happen in New York. So it's off to the City of Angels. Anything could happen in Los Angeles...

I was looking for another angel and found myself swimming with the fishes.

It was September. I was sitting in a dull-colored beige office at the Jules Stein Eye Institute at UCLA, staring out the window. I'd always loved New York in September when the trees and leaves on Fifth Avenue, the whole of Central Park, the Bronx Zoo, and Henry Hudson Parkway turn magical shades of green, yellow and burnt orange.

So what was I doing in Los Angeles? I was about to meet the FISHES and start my quest in the world of make-believe.

The interior of the Eye Institute reminded me of the Uffizi Museum in Florence, Italy, except it didn't contain the hundreds of magnificent pieces of priceless art. It's covered with marble from Carrara, Italy and is very austere looking. Kids got some wicked abrasions as they entertained themselves, sliding across the marble floors while they waited with their parents to have their eyes examined by the young-in training resident physicians in the clinic.

There were three big fishes at the Institute, well, sharks actually. The two killer whites were Jules and Doris Stein, who were always lurking around corners, making unreasonable demands that had nothing to do with quality patient care. They insisted that the Eye Institute building look shining and perfect at all times. This was one of my major responsibilities for which I was generously compensated in addition to my regular UCLA salary.

Fortunately, this need for aesthetics never interfered with good quality patient care. However, they were not an easy duo, so we were always on the lookout—any sighting of these two sharks sent alarm bells throughout the Institute.

One relatively quiet day, an emergency page was sounded. A very distraught Mrs. Stein had to be taken to the X-ray department because she'd slipped and fallen at the airport in Paris, France and may have broken something. She refused treatment in Paris, preferring to come back to UCLA and make OUR lives miserable. Lucky us! Because I was the administrative director and probably the only one not hiding that day, I answered the page and got the "privilege" of escorting her to the Radiology department. While we were waiting for the X-rays to be read, we talked at great length. She wasn't as frightening as she liked to pretend. I liked her, and we became buddies that day...and until I left, we always had a good laugh when she visited, especially about our time together in Radiology.

Doris was the wife of the famed chairman of Universal Studios and Music Corporation of America, Jules Stein and through the years they had contributed a great deal of money to UCLA to create an eye institute. Jules graduated from medical school and trained as an ophthalmologist but never practiced medicine. He went into the band business instead..Smart man.

Here is a perfect example of someone having everything; money, prestige, power and privilege—and yet, in my opinion she was lonely and unhappy.

Then there was the director of the Institute, Bradley R. Straastma. He loved meetings, any kind, any subject. We met every Monday morning, even if there was nothing to meet about. After I left the Institute I swore that I would never have any meetings on Monday mornings. In fact I would never work officially on a Monday either. I have never broken that promise.

Dr. Straastma, a fine physician and excellent surgeon, was fed up with the Steins' constant demands about the physical appearance of the Institute and their apparent lack of interest in patient care. Unfortunately for him, he believed that the "end justifies the means," and wanted more than anything else to direct the Institute. He put up with the misdirected priorities of the Steins. In fairness to Straastma, I think he wanted to create the greatest Eye Institute in the world and so whatever it took, he tolerated. Jules hounded him about the marble polishing, light bulbs over the artwork, bushes trimmed, and how often a copper replica of his head, which was on display near the entrance to the clinic, was polished.

During one of our Monday-morning meetings, Stein called. The conversation was obviously distasteful for Dr. Straastma because, while he held the phone in his right hand, he bent his gold Cross pen in the other. I challenge you to try that. Almost impossible, especially with one hand and small fingers.

Life at the Institute was insane. You had to learn to swim with these sharks or you'd drown. One of Dr. Straastma's assistants, the other shark, a baby shark, but none the less, just as lethal, had been at UCLA too long.

She got great satisfaction in being totally unpleasant and difficult to all of the residents in ophthalmology.

For instance, she would lock their paychecks up in her desk drawer if the resident didn't pick it up by 5pm on Friday. This meant that these poor guys couldn't get paid until Monday morning.

She had no respect for what the residents did, no comprehension about patient care. Residents usually married right after medical school because they couldn't afford to live on their meager salaries. Their weekly paychecks were very important to them. When I tried to explain that Fridays were the busiest day of the week and that it was impossible for residents to pick up their checks before 5pm, she'd twist her face with a despicable smirk and walk away. I wanted to smack her, but I swam instead. I tried reasoning with her but she taught me another lesson of life for which I'm eternally grateful: the one where you know that sometimes there is no reasoning with an unreasonable person, especially a dangerous baby shark.

So I took the matter into my own capable hands. One Friday night, after I found out that one of our most dedicated residents would have to go home without his check, I smashed open her desk with a trusty little hammer that I kept in my desk drawer for such emergencies. I'll never forget the startled look on the resident's face as I handed him his well-deserved check. He was pale and shaking and attempted to gasp out a "thank you" as he ran down the hallway and out the front door. Today he is one of the most successful ophthalmologists in California. The checks were never locked up again. I wonder if he ever remembers that night.

The best part of working at the Institute were the friends I made, especially the two remarkable people who became my cherished friends. Jerry, an extraordinary surgeon who played the spinet, collected ancient Greek and Roman coins, adored Bach and performed cataract surgery faster than any other ophthalmic surgeon.

It was Jerry who named me "The Godmother." "You have 200 employees, you wheel and deal, you make things happen, you're Italian…what else would I call you?" And dear Connie, a beautiful, talented creature whose femininity, charm, and diplomacy made me one of the most successful Administrators at UCLA.

The three of us spent many nights, drinking martinis on the rocks and sharing our dreams while we waited for the traffic gridlock to unlock around UCLA, so we could wind our way home,

It was on one of those nights that I just blurted it out. "My soul is dying! I came out here to be a writer. I have a typewriter and a blank piece of paper, and I haven't typed a word in nine years!"

Jerry laughed hysterically. "What are you talking about?

You're the Godmother. You fix people. You embrace them in good times and bad. You bury yourself in people's lives. You listen! You act.. You're living your story. What more do you want?"

Who knows where it came from? Maybe it was divine intervention. Maybe it was because we were on our second pitcher of martinis, but out of nowhere, Jerry looked at me and said, "Cooking." After several moments of dead silence, he added, "Let's do a Godmother— a delicious food shop in Malibu!" By the end of the evening, a trifle buzzed, we came to the conclusion that The Godmother could happen. I would "handle" the customers, Connie would deal with the money and Jerry would cook. It seemed to make perfect sense, expecially plied with those delicious martinis and a burning desire to get away from the "sharks".

Since I was able to crawl, my life has centered around food. The good times, the bad times. Eating always seemed to make people happy, and happiness heals. Why not?!

PICNICS AND PIES

Our first and unfortunately last Jules Stein Eye Institute family picnic was a month after "The Godmother" idea was conceived. Jerry had been diagnosed with throat cancer, but insisted on coming despite his frail condition. Everyone planned to make his day unforgettable, and it certainly was.

The pie contest was supposed to be just that—a contest with beautiful-looking, mouth-watering pies. We had to get extra tables for the unexpected number of entries. Five judges(from our cast of characters who worked at the Institute) walked the length of the tables, tasting pies and using spoonfuls of sorbet to cleanse their palates in between bits.

All of a sudden, the pies were flying. What started as a nice summer day picnic in the park became a very long, and very messy pie fight . Staff against physicians. Ophthalmologists are usually a quiet bunch, but not this day. Retinal surgeons were pitted against nurses and clerks in the clinic, who were rubbing cherries in the hair of cataract experts. We laughed so hard that we had to roll around on the grass to stop the aching in our stomachs.

The Steins and the Straastmas left early—they were a bit uncomfortable with strawberries, chocolate, meringue and cream flying through the air. They didn't even stop to say goodbye as they ran to their cars.

I knew that I would hear about "the unfortunate incident" first thing Monday morning. I didn't care. It was well worth it, even if I got fired.

Jerry was beyond thrilled. He was glowing, and so was I, but for different reasons. No matter how much I washed, I had blueberry, apple and lemon meringue pie in my hair for weeks afterward.

The "powers" at the Institute found no humor in our gaiety. THAT Monday morning, when we arrived at the Institute, we found a memo on all of our desks......canceling any plans for a second annual picnic. Well, so be it. Jerry died and everything changed anyway. I left to find our dream.

Connie became a mother.

Both of her children, Jake and Jessica are well-adjusted and happy adults. Connie currently lives in the Washington State with her current husband Thomas, still looking for her rainbow and I have the gift of seeing her once or twice a year.

When I left the Institute I was determined to follow Jerry's advice. "Open the Godmother of Malibu." To this day, when I brush my hair, I smell Blueberry and Cream and always remember my two dear friends.

BLUEBERRY PIE

INGREDIENTS:

1 unbaked 10-inch pie shell with top crush: see menu.

FILLING

3 cups	fresh or frozen (unthawed) blueberries
1 ¼ cups	sugar
1 tbs.	sugar (yes, again)
3 tbs.	quick-cooking tapioca
1 tbs.	lemon juice
1/2 tsp.	cinnamon
1 tbs.	butter

DIRECTIONS:

Preheat oven to 400^0.

In a bowl, mix together blueberries, 1 ¼ cups sugar, lemon juice and tapioca.

Pour into unbaked pie shell.

Sprinkle with cinnamon and dot with butter.

Cover withtop crust, flute edges, and vent top with fork.

Sprinkle top crust with 1 tablespoon sugar and bake for 40 to 50 minutes.

If crust starts to darken before the pie is done, cut foil strips to lay over the edges.

(Use pastry crust on page 75)

OLD FASHIONED APPLE PIE

<u>PASTRY</u>:

2 ½ cups	flour
1 tsp.	salt
½ cub	unsalted butter
2	eggs, lightly beaten
½ tbs.	sugar
1 cup	ice water

<u>FILLING</u>:

7	very tart apples
3 tbs.	flour
12 tbs.	sugar
1/2 tsp.	ground cinnamon
Pinch of salt	
2 pinches	ground nutmeg
2 tbs.	cold butter

For the pastry. Mix together flour and salt in a large bowl. Mix in butter and stir until it blends. Sprinkle ice water as you stir dough.

Press dough into a ball, cover and refrigerate.

Preheat oven to 400⁰. Allow dough to sit at room temperature to soften before rolling out on a lightly floured surface.

Place into 9" pie plates...

Peel, quarter and core apples and slice about ¼" thick. In a large mixing bowl place apples, flour, sugar, cinnamon, salt and nutmeg.. Toss until apples are coated. Transfer to pie plate and cover with remaining pastry. Fold edges under and crimp edges. Brush pastry with beaten egg. Make slits about 1" on top pastry for steam to rise. Bake until golden brown, about 1 hour....Lower to 350⁰ if it starts to brown too quickly

LEMON MERINGUE PIE

PASTRY:

3 cups of flour

Pinch of salt

1 1/3 cups of shortening

1 large egg, beaten

1 tbs. vinegar

5 tbs. ice water

FILLING:

1 cup sugar

4 tbs. cornstarch

pinch of salt

2 cups hot water

3 egg yolks, slightly beaten

Juice and grated rind of two lemons

Blend sugar, cornstarch, and salt. Add hot water. Cook 1 minute stirring constantly. Add egg yolks, lemon juice, and rind. Continue cooking for two-three minutes. Cool. Pour into crust.

MERINGUE:

6 tbs. of sugar

3 egg whites

pinch of baking powder

Blend together until stiff. Spread over filling.

Bake 20 minutes at 300^0.

6-8 Servings

BLACKBERRY PIE

PASTRY:

2 cups of flour

2 tbs. of sugar

pinch of salt

1 cup of iced cold butter, cut into small squares

4 tbs. vegetable shortening

1 egg, beaten

FILLING:

6 eggs

1 ¼ cup of sugar

3 cups of blackberries

6 tbs. heavy cream

1 lemon

Mix flour, sugar and salt into a large bowl, and then add butter and shortening.

Add ice water and stir dough. Press dough into a ball, transfer to lightly floured surface, flatten with your hand and make a round.

Wrap dough in plastic wrap and refrigerate for at least 2 hours.

Preheat oven to 400°

Roll dough into a round 14" and fit into a 12" pie pan. Prick bottom with fork. Run rolling pin over rim to remove overhanging dough. Line dough with dried beans or pie weights and bake until crust is set and edges begin to color…about 20 minutes.

Reduce oven temperature to 350⁰, remove weights and brush with egg and continue baking until crust is golden brown....15-20 Minutes

Mix together eggs and sugar in a bowl until pale yellow. Puree 1 ½ cups berries in a blender and stir into egg mixture. Remove zest from ½ of lemon, add to egg mixture. Add cream, mix well.

Arrange remaining berries on bottom of crust, pour in filling and bake until filling is set...about 40 minutes.

Cool before serving..

THE GREATEST GIFT....FRIENDSHIP

From the moment we met, I knew that we would be friends for the rest of our lives. We've been best friends forever and business partners since the founding of the Godmother in 1980. She's my friend, she's my sister. She's quiet, slightly introverted, with extraordinary skills and a close connection to the world beyond. She believes in life after death, and I believe in ghosts...I am an extrovert with an innate business sense, a near perfect intuition and a passion for good food. Are we perfect together or what?

Marlys came from a warm and wonderful Minnesota farm family who relocated to Los Angeles before she was born. Her parents loved each other and remained married all of their lives. This kind of happiness is not very common in Los Angeles. Actually, it's not very common anywhere.

We met when she applied for a three-to-eleven shift at Los Robles Hospital in Thousand Oaks, California. I moved from New York to open this new facility. We bonded immediately. Marlys told me that her marriage wasn't working. She needed a place to stay.

She and the kids, Duane and Val moved in and stayed twenty-five years. She became my anchor, and I her oar. I had an instant family for life. Marlys knew exactly what to do when Jerry died—she got me into the kitchen and we started cooking, using the kids and dogs as our taste-testers.

They reached out and made me a part of their family from day one. Her mother and father became my adoptive parents. They even took me along on their most enjoyed adventures, camping. I'll never forget my first camping experience.

The closest this New Yorker ever came to trees and rolling hills, streams and lakes, roughing it as such, was Central Park. Cooking over a fire meant baking potatoes in the Bronx lot. So this was certainly going to be a new experience. Once we (exaggerated a bit with the "we" they did all the work. I observed with admiration and awe) set up camp, I told grandpa that I'd go to the town's general store to get the firewood. He smiled and said quietly, "Not today, DeeDee. We'll have the raccoons help us." Incredible! The raccoons actually cut the wood. As hard as I tried, however, I couldn't get them to lug it back to camp. This camping stuff was hard work but after three relaxing weeks, I was hooked. We camped outside of Bridgeport, a beautiful region in Northern California, near the High Sierras, with picture-perfect streams from mountain run-off and air clearer than ice.

I learned how to catch trout out of ice cold steams. The kids had to put the bait on the pole, however, and then unhooked the fish for me. I couldn't bear to touch the bate or hurt the fish. We caught one hundred and eleven trout among the six of us. We ate trout for breakfast, lunch and dinner. It was divine. Another life adventure, I shall never forget. If you do nothing else in your life, go camping at least once, in a tent. This was the only vacation I ever had where I lost weight.

It was shocking returning to civilization, and Los Angeles after those incredible three weeks. There were more people everywhere, more than when we left.

Since we've opened the doors to The Godmother, the most popular dish and most consistently requested item is our Tomato Bisque soup. This soup recipe came to Marlys in a dream (from the Angels she says) about the time we opened the shop on Cross Creek Road. She visualized each of the ingredients and all of the instructions. At first, I thought she had smoked some weed (she never had before) Always a first time, I thought. She hadn't though. Marlys is probably clairvoyant and this recipe from "above" just reaffirmed that for me. No kidding just fact. Taste the soup and see that it is different from anything you're ever had before.

For years now, it has been impossible to duplicate this soup outside of the Godmother compound, using all the ingredients according to specific instructions... At The Godmother, Tomato Bisque is always the same in taste and consistency. Despite the fact that tomatoes vary and no two cooks are the same, it's always the same. That's the mystery. The recipe is here. Now in this book. You may be able to conquer the 'curse', but don't blame me if you don't.

Marlys has had many dreams of foods. Many of them have inspired recipes which are now Godmother standards, but none more popular than the Tomato Bisque. More about dreams and food later.

THREE THINGS IN LIFE ARE IMPORTANT:
THE FIRST IS TO BE KIND.
THE SECOND IS TO BE KIND.
THE THIRD IS TO BE KIND.

—HENRY JAMES

EGGS BILLIE GAY

I repeat, in my family it was the natural order of the universe to always have deliciously tasting and healthy food for all of our meals; breakfast, lunch and dinner. On holidays, eating was even more special because of the involvement of the entire family and their desire to show off their culinary talents. Good food surrounded us all of the time. We never had to think about food.........it was there...always.

Not in Billie Gay's family. Food was unimportant. They ate to live, not lived to eat, like us.. They were poor when she was a youngster, and so they struggled to keep food on the table. There was very little thought to quality.

Billie Gay thought of food as an interruption of her daily routine. I didn't know it then, but she had very little variety in her diet mostly steak, eggs, pizza, cheese and salads.

Once in awhile she threw in some fruit. That's probably why she had so much energy—all that protein. She was rail-thin and moved faster than the speed of sound.

Although Billie Gay was a Southerner, she talked and moved just like a New Yorker. The first time I ate dinner at her home, she asked the lovely hispanic housekeeper-cook to broil a couple of steaks. A couple of martinis later, we were looking at a gray piece of meat with edges curled up on our plates. The housekeeper heard "boil." Not wanting to hurt her feelings, Billie Gay thanked her, threw the steaks to the dogs, and we sneaked out of the house to a nearby restaurant.

She was born Wilma Gay Estes. In Kentucky, her family took in washing for both the white and black families in their small town and worked round the clock to get out of there and give both her and her sister a good education. They succeeded. She graduated with honors from Emory University in Georgia.

She was indeed one of a kind—a wonderful, whimsical Southerner who could talk you into and out of anything in record speed, with a great deal of charm. We met when I was asked by a friend and former boss from New York to take over her job as personnel director at Queen of Angels Hospital in Los Angeles. My friend was taking a six-month sabbatical and needed me to cover for her. I was living in San Francisco at the time, but I was tired of Tony Bennett's song and those damned fog horns. I was in San Francisco when John F. Kennedy was assassinated and the world went nuts.. The fog horns never stopped that horrible weekend.

Sunny Southern California sounded so delicious and refreshing and so I jumped at the chance to see another part of California.

Billie Gay was the director of nursing. The only instructions my friend gave me about the job was that given my experience, I'd adjust easily to everything but working with Billie Gay. She was a definite challenge.

On my first day, I found her eating breakfast in the hospital cafeteria. She had poured an entire shaker of salt on top of her eggs. I couldn't see the yolks. She laughed when she saw the curious expression on my face. "I'm not crazy about eggs, so the salt helps," she said. Odd, but as I got to know her better, her many little quarks seemed quite logical. We became best friends instantly.

Sometime and somewhere during the next couple of years, while I was back on the East Coast, she married Bill Hall, M.D. Nobody quite knows exactly where and when. They had four terrific kids. When I wanted to return to L.A., I told the Halls that I had to live by the water. Billie Gay and Bill helped me find my home in Malibu. Bill scaled heights, hanging very precariously over the ocean on railings or decks to see what for-sale houses on the beach looked like on the inside. Or he'd hang off sides of mountains when I thought maybe living in the Canyon would work. He was fearless and thank God I found the right house before he fell into a bottomless canyon or out to sea.

Billie Gay was a magician with money. She was very California real-estate savvy before California real-estate savvy was in. She bought orange and lime ranches in Vista, that became the juice capital of the West. She bought a beach house in Carpenteria when people asked where that was. She could smell good investments miles away and she smelled The Godmother. She could turn straw into gold with her charm. She did it with people places and things. She did it with me. She did it for The Godmother.

Every year, she held a tennis and golf tournament in Palm Springs, for over 100 of her closest friends and neighbors. One year, after a very wild party (nothing we'd be ashamed of other than too much drinking), we needed a breakfast that would cure our hangovers. Searching the refrigerator, we found eggs, chilis and cheese, and created "Eggs Billie Gay." Adding a few ingredients through the years to spice it up, it is now one of the Godmother's most requested entreés and is the star at our annual Mother's Day Brunch.

EGGS BILLIE GAY

INGREDIENTS:

½ lb. cheddar cheese, shredded

½ lb. jack cheese, shredded

28 oz. can whole green chilies, drained & seeded

8 large eggs

½ cup cream

DIRECTIONS:

Preheat oven to 350°.

Spray an 8x8 baking dish with vegetable spray. Layer the bottom of the baking dish with half of the seeded green chilies. Mix the two shredded cheeses together and place half of the cheese on top of the green chili layer.

Next add another layer of green chilies, and top this layer with the remaining shredded cheese.

Crack the 8 eggs into a blender and add the cream. Blend for 2 minutes on high.

Pour eggs mixture over the cheese and chilies and place in 350° oven for 50-60 minutes, until mixture is set and top is golden brown.

Serves 6

ONE CANNOT
THINK WELL, LOVE WELL, SLEEP WELL,
IF ONE HAS NOT DINED WELL.

—VIRGINIA WOOLF

ON THE ROAD & GUACAMOLE

Morningview Drive is a conservative, affluent neighborhood in La Canada, California, set against the San Gabriel Mountains. The most exciting thing to happen on that street was the Hall family.

Some people have to create drama to be happy. The Hall family's drama came out of their happiness. That was Billie Gay's charm. I loved being a part of it. I could have never guessed that one of Billie Gay's craziest weekend adventures would become the inspiration for the birth of The Godmother.

It was a Saturday morning when Billie Gay invited Marlys, the kids, the dogs and me over for a swim and a barbecue. I should've known that the invitation sounded much too normal for the Halls. I was right.

Five minutes after we arrived at their home, we were all wearing those ridiculous sombreros and serapes. When Bill arrived home from the hospital (he was an E.N.T surgeon), Billie Gay had already thrown the kids and the dogs in the Winnebago and blended pitchers of margaritas. Bill ripped off his tie, dipped a chip in homemade guacamole, yelled for us to jump aboard and off we went. We had no clue that Mexico was where Billie Gay had planned to have our swim and barbecue.

We laughed, we swam, we fished and we ate a lot. Our culinary creations were blooming between the chilled martinis and the nightly fish sauces we created. Bill cooked our fresh fish on the fire-pit made of beach rocks. We ate delicious fish meals on the beach every night carefully sprinkled with our sauces.

On our way home Billie Gay convinced me that it was time for The Godmother to be born...even if we had to put it on wheels. "What wheels".

Two days later, we were on our way to Carson, a scary neighborhood in the belly of L.A. It's the place where catering vans are built and sold. After scouring several lots, we spotted it. It looked so big to me, 20 feet of white and shining metal on "wheels". "I'll be damn". This is what she meant.

Billie Gay paid cash right on the spot, and convinced the dealer to throw in the lettering. We waited, not very patiently, but we waited.

Hours later, the van appeared, "The Godmother" lettered in black on both sides. Here we go again, I thought, another adventure with Billie Gay. We had to get this monster home to Malibu. While I was making suggestions like let's do some practice driving and get used to the many lights, knobs and switches that this thing had on the dash board, Billie Gay jumped inside, hit the gas and took off.

She was headed towards the Santa Monica Freeway. I could barely keep up, pushing the jet engines of her brand new Lincoln Continential as much as they would take. Fortunately, she hit a bit of traffic and slowed down so I did catch up for a moment. Motorists that day must have though someone was running for Mayor, or that perhaps a movie was being filmed. Billie Gay stood the entire way home, waving and honking to everyone she passed. I was sure she was going to be pulled over and arrested for endangering the lives of anyone who got in her way. But people seemed to love it, trying to get a better look at this beautiful blonde driving erratically in this big, white van with huge letters that spelled out 'The Godmother'.

Within days, we leased a small, empty lot on Pacific Coast Highway and decorated the van with balloons and flags. We opened for business the next week. All of our kids, six in total, dressed in black Godmother t-shirts with angel wings on the back (what else?), passed out balloons to everyone who stopped, while Callas's Tosca' blared from the speakers atop the van.

We served eighty-six people that day. Miraculously, six of those people actually paid. The other eighty were family and friends. My grandma said that when a bird poops on you, or anything that is yours, it means the angels are bringing you good luck. By the time we got home that first night, the top of the van was covered in bird poop. Twenty seven years later, I gotta say, Grandma was right on!

GUACAMOLE

INGREDIENTS:

10 whole ripe avocados, mashed

2 tbs. lemon juice, freshly squeezed

1 medium onion, finely chopped

6 shakes Tabasco sauce

½ cup fresh salsa

1 tsp. Godmother salt to taste

DIRECTIONS:

Cut avocados in half, hollow out pulp. Save 3 pits.

Place ripe avocado in a small bowl and mash to desired consistency. Add lemon juice, finely chopped onion, salsa, Tabasco sauce, and salt, and mix well.

Place 3 avocado pits in with the guacamole to prevent browning.

Cover and chill till ready to serve.

THE SHOP....ON CROSS CREEK

If I had a dollar for everyone who said that they bought food from the Godmother van when it was parked on Pacific Coast Highway, my dog Sophia and I would be sunbathing on the Piazza dell'Olivetta in Portofino, Italy at this very moment, sipping a strong espresso and eating white figs with fresh, thinly, sliced prosciutto.

On May 17, 1981 we opened the shop on Cross Creek Road in Malibu, a year to the date of opening the van doors on Pacific Coast Highway. No coincidence. I planned it. That date, is also Val's birthday. Cross Creek is famous because it's the main street of downtown Malibu, and at that time, the only place to shop, outside of the large, unattractive supermarkets.

Our shop was smart looking, with warm colors of white and green tables and chairs to match. Everything was shiny and new. We were an instant hit. We offered a different kind of menu, different than just the salads and sandwiches, hot dogs and hamburgers found all over Malibu.

Along with the food came advice and excellent wines poured generously, most of the time free of charge. Our display cases were stocked full of beautiful-looking, carefully decorated foods, which tasted even better than they looked. We offered a wide selection, like nothing ever found in Malibu before. And all this was accompanied by a lot of personality and laughter.

GIVING BACK

IF YOU WANT HAPPINESS
FOR AN HOUR—TAKE A NAP
IF YOU WANT HAPPINESS
FOR A DAY—GO FISHING.
IF YOU WANT HAPPINESS
FOR A MONTH—GET MARRIED.
IF YOU WANT HAPPINESS
FOR A YEAR—INHERIT A FORTUNE
IF YOU WANT HAPPINESS
FOR A LIFETIME—HELP SOMEONE ELSE.

—CHINESE PROVERB

BUFFET OF EVENTS

What a cast of characters we've met during these past twenty-seven years. As I tell some of these stories, I'll use names where it's appropriate. Other stories will contain the true story but no names, for obvious reasons.

If I unintentionally upset anyone with any of these stories, I apologize. This is not a tell-all book. It's a storybook about food and friendship, and what happened to a little shop on a little street in a little town called Malibu. The Chinese have a saying, "Food is a way of communicating love and friendship." So it happens that my second-favorite food is Chinese ... so I believe anything Chinese, especially the part about love and friendship.

These past years have been thrilling. I've met such an assortment of people; such a mixed bag; a lot of celebrities; some just plain folk; many strange birds who didn't exactly beat to the same drummer, brilliant minds, and some duller than a stack of hammers, but all of them have left a mark. It's been an interesting ride and a wonderful adventure for me. If you don't find this book gripping, engrossing, absorbing, exciting, riveting or unputdownable, don't dispair, the recipes are great!!!!!

Those handmade wooden screen doors at The Godmother Shop on Cross Creek opened and closed with a string of different and unique personalities from the day we opened. These people have become friends, and part of my extended family.

The Godmother has participated in the most important times of their lives. Births, deaths, birthdays, baby's firsts, sweet sixteens, centennials, bar mitzvahs, anniversaries, weddings, divorces, Valentine's Day, Easter, Mother's Day, Memorial Day, the Fourth of July, Labor Day, Halloween, Thanksgiving, Christmas, New Year's, the Super Bowl, Chanukah, Yom Kippur, Passover, National Quilt Day and so many, many pet birthdays.

We shared our hearts and our talents and entered their worlds. We became a part of their lives, and although some have moved from Malibu, the memories will last forever.

OH, YES ZUCCHINI PIE....

Mike McCann is one of the foremost young men who was raised in Malibu.. Those who know him and love him will attest to how he figured out when he was five years old that I, The Godmother can't make a "very good" godmother sandwich. He's never been quite sure why and I have never told him until now ... "It's all in the preparation Mike." The mechanics of putting a godmother sandwich together demands extraordinary patience. Enough said!

Each piece of cold cut/or cheese must be laid singularly onto the roll ... very specifically. You never add the salami before you add the cheese for instance ... makes the difference between a "very good" godmother sandwich and an "okay" godmother sandwich. Mike rates mine as "okay" and Mike and his brother Kevin, another 'topper' of a guy ate my sandwiches for years without complaining. Anyone else who made this sandwich got much higher marks than I ever did.

These guys know good food. And so they should, because there mother is Roxanne, whose daily routine for years included a visit to the shop on Cross Creek. She's a terrific cook and considered this town's expert on our Zucchini Pie. She's eaten it every day for years.

She can even tell after the first bite who made the pie that day. We call it befittingly, on our menu Roxanne's Zucchini Pie.

The 'pie' is not really a 'pie' in the true sense of the word. It's a torta which was created by my Aunt Emma. As a young woman, she couldn't boil water. My mother pitied her and said, "you'll never get out of the Bronx, unless you learn how to cook," and proceeded to teach her the basics. She became a very adept cook and the Zucchini Pie became a family staple. Up until the day she died, at 92, my dear, flamboyant Aunt Emma had her hair done and nails polished weekly and was still cooking luscious meatballs and Zucchini Pie. She leaves us the legacy of the Zucchini Pie which is a mouthful of pleasure.

"I've spent the best part of my life at The Godmother", Roxanne has said. And that she has. Squeezed in between her marriage to Austin, who I wish I could zerox (he's almost the perfect man) her two boys, her joys, her sadnesses (the loss of her wonderful dad, her mom and her brother) plus so many dear friends.

There are so many McCann stories. One of my favorites is about the band 'URGE'. When Mike was ten years old, he and his best pal, Johnny along with their pals, Ambrose and Nicholas formed the band 'URGE'. They were desperate to perform in public. The Godmother opened the Café for their first ever concert. Hundreds of kids from their Malibu school attended, along with their parents. The band performed their own music and was introduced to the crowd and the local television cable channel by the former great rock star of the Jefferson Airplane and Jefferson Starship, Grace Slick. Most of those ten and eleven year olds had no clue who Grace was but the mom's and dad's and their friends sure did and figured they got a steal for the five buck admission fee.

ROXANNE'S ZUCCHINI PIE

INGREDIENTS:

3 small zucchini, thinly sliced

1 medium onion, finely chopped

4 large eggs

½ cup parmesan cheese

½ cup canola oil

1 cup Bisquick baking mix

1/8 tsp. black pepper

DIRECTIONS:

Spray an 8x8, 2 ½" deep baking pan with a vegetable spray, or brush with canola oil.

Thinly slice zucchini and set aside.

In a medium size bowl, add the 4 eggs, the finely chopped onion, Bisquick, parmesan cheese, canola oil and black pepper. Mix well by hand (do not over beat).

Fold the thinly sliced zucchini into the Bisquick till well-covered. Pour the mixture into the greased baking pan.

Place in a 350° preheated oven for 40 to 60 minutes, till top is golden brown and a knife stuck in the center comes out clean.

Serves 4

WITH MEATLOAF COMES LOVE....

Another one of my favorite characters left this earth much too soon.

Saturdays were special on Cross Creek because Lenny and his wife Susan came to just hang out with us. They were a very funny couple, making us laugh a lot as we tried to feed half of Malibu. It was pure East Coast Jewish humor. Eating was their avocation and watching the scenery roll by while they sipped their cappuccinos was their favorite weekend activity.....in addition to loading up on take-out foods to stack their cupboards for the week.

We catered all of their parties... and we never did a party without somehow including the turkey meatloaf.

Lenny was obsessed with our meat loaf, often eating it for breakfast, lunch and dinner. So it was so natural for Susan to want his favorite food served at his memorial reception.

It was a touching memorial, sad because he was young and full of expectations, but very traditional and very spiritual with all of the foods usually served at a Jewish service including lox, bagels, white fish, sour cream, knishes, and ..smack in the center of all these mouthwatering treats was this huge turkey meatloaf.

During the holidays, we usually ship a Lenny's Meatloaf to his son, who now lives in Chicago ... a beautiful way of remembering his dad.

LENNY'S MEATLOAF

INGREDIENTS:

1 ½ lbs. ground turkey*

2 cups French bread, broken into pieces

¼ cup cream

2 large eggs, broken

1 medium onion, chopped fine

1 medium green bell pepper, chopped, seeded

½ cup Parmesan cheese

¼ cup barbeque sauce

1 tsp. garlic, minced

½ tsp. basil

½ tsp. oregano

¼ tsp. sage

2 tsps. Godmother salt

2 tsps. pepper

2 tsps. Worcestershire sauce

2 tbs. barbecue sauce, brushed on top

DIRECTIONS:

Preheat oven to 375⁰.

In a medium-ize mixing bowl, add the torn pieces of french bread, cream, eggs, and ground turkey. Continue to add the chopped onion, green bell pepper, parmesan cheese, barbecue sauce, Worcestershire sauce, basil, oregano, sage, salt and pepper.

Mix all Ingredients together till well-blended.

LENNY'S MEATLOAF
(CONTINUED)

Place mixture into an oblong baking dish and shape into an oblong loaf.

Brush top of meatloaf with 2 tablespoons of barbeque sauce.

Bake at 375⁰ for 1 hour.

Serves 4

* You can use ground beef if you'd like.

"LET THEM BRING THEIR OWN LUNCH"

The movie theater audience was still but you could feel the movement – the quiet stirring, the coughs, chewing, sipping, whispers.

Up on the screen, the camera, which is focused on a magnificent moon in the sky, pans to a bedroom. The very gifted and sarcastically funny actress Olympia Dukakis, who is playing Cher's mother, says to Cher (playing Loretta in the movie Moonstruck), after she hears of Loretta's engagement, "Do you love him, Loretta?"

Loretta replies, "No Ma, I don't."

"That's good because if you love 'em, they break your heart."

A classic tale of real family life. I adore that movie. It reminds me of one continuous Sunday dinner at Grandma's. The movie, directed by the very talented Norman Jewison, comforts me and fills my heart with memories of my Italian family in the Bronx.

Norman, his warm, generous and sometimes hilarious wife Dixie, and their kids, Jenny, David, (Jenny's husband) Michael and Kevin have been customers and friends since the first week we opened. We catered so many family and social events for them. Dixie's telephone call to The Godmother would alert us to the date of her event. Whenever I'd ask how many people she was expecting, she'd say, "I don't call anyone until I check to see if you're available." You'd think after twenty + years, I'd have known not to ask that question. I think I just liked the way she came back at me with that reply.

We did every type of event imaginable. The Jewison's are Canadian and so if they were in Malibu on Canadian Independence Day, we were challenged with creating interesting menus with maple syrup imported from their own farm in Toronto. They even had Canadian Mounted Police, (Mounties) compliments of the Canadian Embassy, stationed at their front door when the Canadian prime minister was the guest of honor. The Mounties, who appeared wooden, really had some warmth within. They cracked a smile when we offered them some Canadian popovers. However, they eat without moving their lips. No kidding.

We served gazpacho and tea sandwiches when the Jewison's hosted a tea for the Ontario Gallery for the Arts. We served borscht to the Russians at the cultural exchange dinner. Thanks to Dixie and Norman we created and still use a wide variety of international menu ideas.

Dixie's personal favorite, our curried chicken salad served with fresh coconut, mango chutney, chopped nuts and a side of jasmine rice was the mainstay at her yearly ladies luncheon.

We served it so often that I suggested humorously once, that if she wanted to keep serving the same menu, she might consider changing her guest list. Always quick with the response, she replied,

"Let them bring their own lunch if they are unhappy." No one ever complained.

Everyone always raved about that menu. And she never changed one part of it nor one guest.

Dixie Jewison died on Thanksgiving Day, 2004.

At her Memorial Service, guests were served Dixie's curried chicken salad as a special tribute to this very special lady. I will miss her forever.

DIXIE'S CURRIED CHICKEN SALAD

INGREDIENTS:

6 medium chicken breasts halves without skin

1 cup orange juice

¼ cup olive oil

¼ cup cilantro, chopped

½ cup mayonnaise

2 tbs. mango chutney, chopped fine

½ tsp. curry powder

1 tbs. sweet sherry

¾ cup celery, chopped fine

1 cup seedless grapes, cut in half

¼ cup slivered almonds, toasted

½ cup mango chutney, as a condiment

½ cup toasted coconut, as a condiment

½ cup toasted chopped almonds, as a condiment

DIRECTIONS:

In a medium-size baking dish marinate the boneless, skinless chicken breast in the orange juice, olive oil and chopped cilantro. Marinate for 4 hours or overnight in the refrigerator.

Heat a cast iron skillet or a pancake griddle, brush with olive oil and grill the six chicken breasts, 3 to 4 minutes on each side, until juice runs clear. Set aside until cool. Then cut into 1 inch pieces.

DIXIE'S CURRIED CHICKEN SALAD
(CONTINUED)

In a medium size bowl place the chopped chicken, the finely chopped celery, the grape halves, and the toasted almonds, and toss until well-coated with the dressing.

THE DRESSING:

In a small bowl, whisk together the mayonnaise, mango chutney, curry powder and sherry. Serve at room temperature or chilled.

Serve with condiments which can be placed on top of chicken salad or on side.

Serves 6

JASMINE COCONUT RICE

INGREDIENTS:

2 cups Jasmine rice, washed

3 cups chicken broth

¼ cup coconut, shredded

2 tbs. fresh mint, minced

1 tbs. fresh basil, minced

DIRECTIONS:

In a medium saucepan, bring 3 cups of chicken broth to a boil, stir in the 2 cups of Jasmine rice, cover. Simmer on low for 20 minutes.

Remove from heat, let stand for 10 minutes.

Uncover, stir in coconut, mint and basil. Stir with a fork to fluff.

Place rice in a serving dish, garnish with a sprig of mint.

Great served with poultry or fish. And especially Dixie's curried chicken.

Serves 6

PASTA AND MORE PASTA....

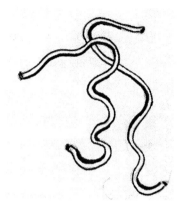

Larry Hagman's fiftieth birthday party was a Texas-sized event. Very appropriate, since the entire cast and crew, along with his family and local friends from his hit television program 'Dallas' were there.

The most difficult part in the planning of this party was convincing the hostess that we needed a lot of food for 100 people. I'd rather eat glass than run out of food. I knew the possibility of running out of food was a distinct possibility. Because I knew my mother would swing a large wooden spoon down from heaven and smack me over the head if this happened, I decided to work a bit of diplomacy, (not an easy road for me but drastic situations call for drastic measures.)

The Hagmans lived a stone's throw away from the shop, so I decided that I could watch the bowls very carefully and when they started to get low, I'd run over to the shop, where I left pots on the stove on a slow boil, whip up a batch and be back before anyone knew the difference.

Most of the cast and crew looked as though they were ten feet tall, and they had matching appetites. The minute I saw the rush to the buffet table, I knew I'd be heading back to the pots. No one even knew I was gone for a half hour, and the buffet line just kept going and going. The meal continued without a lost breath…except mine.

I met some delightful people that night. This was one of my first big-time celebrity parties, and I was so happy to hear conversations about art, music, theater, kids, baseball, Texas and Pacific Coast Highway… Normal conversations, not "what do you think of my new gown or diamonds or face lift?

Stars and crew mixed with other guests as easily as strawberries and crème. They all seemed to like each other, and certainly liked Larry… but what's not to like about Larry?

PASTA WITH BROCCOLI RABE

INGREDIENTS:

1 lb. Orchiette pasta

3 cups of parmesan cheese

1 ¼ cups of extra virgin olive oil

8 shallots, minced

6 tbs. chopped garlic

½ cup dry sherry

1/2 lb. of butter

2 tsp. Godmother seasoned salt

5 bunches of broccoli rabe

DIRECTIONS:

Cook pasta in large pot with approximately 4 quarts of water. (al dente "tender but firm to the bite")

Drain and toss with olive oil and 2 cups parmesan cheese until well coated.

Set aside.

In large pan add shallots, garlic, olive oil, dry sherry, butter, Godmother's seasoned salt and sauté until shallots are clear.

Add bunches of broccoli rabe, braise for 5-8 more minutes and toss with the pasta. Add the last cup of parmesan cheese.

Serves 6

LINGUINI GRECO

INGREDIENTS:

½ lb. linguini

½ lb. spinach linguini

¾ cup black olives, drained and sliced

3 green onions, sliced

3 Roma tomatoes, chopped

½ lb. feta cheese, crumbled

¼ cup parsley, chopped

¾ cup olive oil

2 lemons, juiced

1 tsp. oregano

½ tsp. black pepper

DIRECTIONS:

Add both pastas to 8 quarts of boiling salted water, cook until ("al dente" tender but firm to the touch), 8 – 10 minutes. Drain and rinse in cold water 2 to 3 times, and place in a medium bowl.

Add sliced black olives, sliced green onions and chopped Roma tomatoes to the pasta, and toss.

THE DRESSING:

In a small bowl, add olive oil, oregano and black pepper. Slowly whisk in lemon juice until well blended.

Pour dressing over pasta, toss until well coated.

Place in a serving bowl and top with crumbled feta cheese and chopped parsley. Chill 1 hour before serving.

SERVES 6

RED BEAN SALAD

INGREDIENTS:

1 16 oz. can kidney beans

2 stalks celery, diced

1 small green bell pepper, chopped

1 small red bell pepper, chopped

2 green onions, chopped

¼ cup parsley, chopped

¼ cup fresh basil, chopped

2 tsp. capers

THE DRESSING:

½ cup olive oil

1 lemon, juice of

½ tsp. Tabasco sauce

DIRECTIONS:

Drain kidney beans and place in a medium bowl.

To bowl of kidney beans, add diced celery, chopped green and red bell peppers, chopped green onions, chopped parsley, chopped fresh basil and one tablespoon of capers.

In a small bowl combine lemon juice, Tabasco sauce and whisk in olive oil.

Pour dressing over beans and vegetables. Mix and toss until well coated. Chill for 1 hour

Serves 6

CAESAR SALAD

INGREDIENTS:

2 heads romaine lettuce

2 cups croutons, freshly made

½ cup grated parmesan cheese

¼ cup lemon juice, freshly squeezed

2 tsp. garlic, minced

6 filets anchovies, minced

¾ cup olive oil, whisk in

a pinch of sugar, whisk in

1 tsp. Worcestershire sauce, whisk in

black pepper to taste, freshly ground

DIRECTIONS:

Wash and pat dry 2 heads of romaine lettuce, several hours before serving.

THE DRESSING:

In a small mixing bowl, add the lemon juice, the minced garlic, minced anchovies, pinch of sugar, and Worcestershire sauce. Whisk in the olive oil until fully mixed, set aside.

In a salad bowl, tear the middle and inner leaves of romaine into bite-size pieces. Gently toss with Caesar salad dressing, parmesan cheese and croutons.

Top with freshly ground pepper.

May be served with sliced grilled chicken or shrimp on top.

SERVES 6

THE CORPSE WAS RESTLESS

When the mother of a very prominent Los Angeles entertainment attorney died, 300 of his closest friends and colleagues were invited to the memorial and reception, held at the prestigious Westward Presbyterian Church, in Westwood, California.

The buffet featured some of our clients' favorite food such as— grilled chicken couscous, chilled asparagus with ginger dressing, and spinach salad. When my staff was setting up the buffet tables, I noticed a huge portrait of the deceased, leaning against the wall, practically draping the buffet table. Alive or dead, it was depressing. Painted in dark oils, the face was twisted like a pretzel, with not an inkling of a smile and certainly no make up.... Although a solemn occasion, this would really make it worse.

"I can't have this picture near my food.", I thought. "Nobody will eat." I signaled for help, and we moved the "portrait of gloom" to the bar area. "Much better," I thought. With a few drinks, anybody looks good and she will too.

Guests started arriving, so I hurried to the kitchen to make sure that we were set to go. Returning to the dining room a few minutes later, I noticed that the portrait was back in its original spot. How or why was it moved? I didn't know and I didn't care. Quickly, I yelled for my crew, and back it went to the bar.

When it found its way back to the dining room the third time, I gave up. This corpse was restless. I wasn't about to start fooling around with forces I couldn't explain. At least, not before everyone was fed.

The bizarre day continued. When it was time for the internment at the Westwood Cemetery, which was next door to the church, the guests started toward the cemetery which happens to be the final resting place of Marilyn Monroe and Natalie Wood and many other well knowns. Hundreds crowded the sidewalks and the parking lots hoping to see the "live" celebrities in attendance.

"Grab that handle," someone yelled. I obeyed, but to this day, I can't figure out why. I don't even know how I got outside so quickly. We started to move down the street, but suddenly the cart carrying the coffin broke loose and started rolling down a slight grade, picking up speed as it rolled. It was headed west, and I guarantee you it would not have stopped until it reached the Pacific Ocean had a bunch of brave souls not thrown themselves in front of the cart.

The only damage was a few frayed nerves and some scuffed shoes. This corpse was not going to her grave quietly.

I am not a betting woman, but I'd lay odds that this particular corpse comes and goes out of Westward at will.

GRILLED EGGPLANT SALAD

INGREDIENTS:

1 large eggplant, cut into ½" pieces

2 tsp. Godmother salt

1 medium zucchini, chopped into ½" pieces

1 large red bell pepper, cut into ½" pieces

1 large green bell pepper, cut into ½" pieces

1 medium red onion, chopped

4 oz. button mushroom, sliced

½ cup olive oil

4 Roma tomatoes

½ cup fresh basil, chopped

THE DRESSING:

3 tbs. balsamic vinegar

2 tsp. sugar

1 tbs. soy sauce

½ cup olive oil

In a blender, add vinegar, sugar, soy sauce. Blend on high and drizzle in olive oil.

DIRECTIONS:

Grill vegetables 8 to 10 minutes. Toss with the dressing while still hot. Put aside.

When vegetables are at room temperature, toss in 4 Roma tomatoes, cut into ½ inch pieces, and ½ cup fresh basil, also chopped into ½ inch pieces.

Serves 6

GRILLED CHICKEN COUSCOUS

INGREDIENTS:

4 chicken breast halves, boneless and skinless

1 large lemon, juiced

¼ cup extra virgin olive oil for marinade

1 tsp. garlic, minced

1 tbs. fresh oregano, chopped

1 ½ cups of couscous

2 cups chicken broth

1 bunch of green onions

2 tbs. fresh oregano

¼ cup lemon jice

2 tbs. honey

2 tsp. dijon mustard

¾ cup extra virgin olive oil

¼ cup almonds or cashews, toasted

Godmother salt and some pepper to taste

DIRECTIONS:

Bring chicken broth to boil. In a medium size bowl, add couscous, chicken broth, cover and set aside.

Marinate chicken breasts in olive oil, lemon juice, garlic and fresh chopped oregano for at least one hour.

Grill over barbecue or on a hot pancake grill, 3 - 4 minutes each side, let cool.

GRILLED CHICKEN COUSCOUS
(CONTINUED)

Cuisinart green onions and fresh oregano to a medium chop. Put olive oil on grill or in a small fry pan. Brown onions and oregano on both sides. Set aside and cook.

Fluff couscous with a fork. Toss with green onions and fresh oregano.

Cut grilled chicken into thin slices. Make a dressing whisking lemon juice, honey, salt, pepper and olive oil together.

Toss chicken and couscous together with dressing. Top with toasted almonds or cashews.

Serves 6

CHICKEN PASTA

INGREDIENTS:

1 lb. fettuccini

1 lb. fresh chicken breast, diced

4 stalks celery

3 green onions

8 oz. green frozen peas

1 cup mayonnaise

1 ½ cups Chablis

1 tbs. Dijon mustard

½ cup black olives

1 tbs. dill

DIRECTIONS:

Add fettuccini into boiling water. Cook eight – ten minutes. (al dente, of course)

Drain and rinse well in cold water, place in bowl.

In another bowl, add diced chicken, finely sliced green onion, sliced black olives, and frozen peas. Toss together and add to pasta bowl.

THE DRESSING:

In a small bowl, whip together mayonnaise, Chablis, Dijon mustard and dill.

Pour dressing over pasta, toss, and refrigerate for 1 hour.

Serve on a bed of arugula, if you'd like.

Serves 6

KEYS TO HAPPINESS...

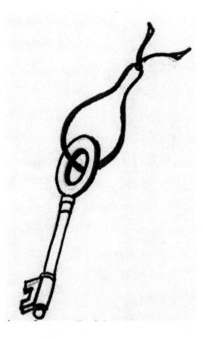

One of my all time favorite actresses and humans is Audrey Hepburn. During a moment on the set of *Breakfast at Tiffany's* she was asked how she kept herself so lovely... somewhat embarrased she responded "I try to be kind, I try to seek out good in people, I always share my food with the hungry, I walk, knowing I'm never alone, and I know that if I need a helping hand, it's never very far away. Those are the keys for my happiness."

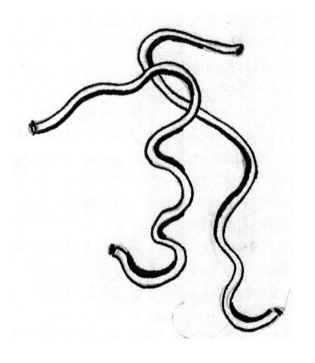

IT'S ADDICTIVE

Cindy Crawford, the supermodel, lived in Malibu for awhile when our shop was located on Cross Creek Road. Cindy is a natural beauty, so it was always refreshing to see her on Saturday mornings. She was delightful, and the shop was a happier place with her presence. Never expecting special treatment, she waited patiently on the long lines that were part of the weekend routine that became a 'Malibu ritual; stocking up the cupboards so that you didn't have to travel Pacific Coast Highway on the summer weekends. (unless it was a dire emergency).

Her favorite purchases were spicy soba noodles along with honey baked chicken and celery root salad. The soba noodles are actually non-fattening because they are made with tahini and buck wheat noodles, they are definately 'less-fattening' than most other noodles.

Leaning over the counter one Saturday, I said "Hey Cindy, do you think if I ate as many soba noodles as you buy, I would get to look like you?" Her face lit up with that infectious smile and her eyes sparkled. "You look pretty terrific to me," she replied. What a generous and kind thing to say to someone who was terribly overweight at the time. She's in a business where you have to be diplomatic most of the time and could have wiggled out of commenting, but she didn't.

My self-esteem is fine but I've struggled with the weight thing for years, and as obvious as this was to everyone, it was a lovely gesture on her part and something I've never forgotten.

I've entertained this idea for years and wishing my higher power would really make it happen ... you know the old saying, "be careful what you wish for" ... oh, how I wish!!!!!!

We should be able to give our extra weight, at will, to those people who piss us off. Wouldn't that be a great stress reliever? These would be my prime targets: The guy, who cuts you off driving recklessly down Pacific Coast Highway or any road, gets thirty pounds right off the bat; the waiter, in an expensive restaurant who doesn't know the menu and could care even less, gets five pounds; the rude broad who stands in line at Starbucks talking loudly on her cell phone at 7am gets twenty-five pounds, right then and there. Maybe anyone who uses a cell phone in a public place, especially when others are trying to serve them should also get twenty-five pounds. I'd be wearing my promised (when I reached a certain clothing size) Armani suit in no time.

I've done it all. I can't really understand my weight fiasco because I swim 1000 meters two or three times a week, walk up and down stairs every day; have a high energy level and even once signed up with 'Curves', where in thirty minutes you complete your exercise by running from one machine to another while you laugh a lot with other women who have the same struggles and listen to more Malibu gossip than I thought could ever be possibe in one town. Ah, but the reality is that losing weight always takes a great sacrifice like giving up ice cream and chocolate cake. Sometimes life isn't fair.

At one stage of my quest for the perfect body, I listened to a client who had great success she claimed, with an allergist in Beverly Hills. Immediately just hearing where he was located told me this was going to be a costly quest. What was I thinking? My failure to lose weight was quite simple. I ate the wrong foods sometimes and ate too much of any foods all the time. I know better but off I went and after hundreds of dollars of tests and what felt like thousands of needles in my back, the 'fat' guru concluded that I was allergic to hog hair. I come from The Bronx, which is in New York, not Mississippi. I don't think I've ever rubbed shoulders with a hog. I found out that hogs are pigs that are older and weigh considerably more than regular pigs. But only in the United States are they called hogs. In Great Britian all domesticated swine is referred to as pigs. So, if I had seen this fat guru in Great Britian I would be allergic to pig hair. "thanks doc for adding yet another layer to my weight misery". And how the hell does that affect my weight anyhow? Our Beverly Hills allergist was at a loss to make me understand. I am sure he smiled all the way to the bank. I decided then and there, never to return to Beverly Hills for anything ever again.

This is what did work.........

Wanting desperately to be around on this earth for a long time to watch my beautiful and precious granddaughter, Kailani Kea grow up. (she was born on March 5, 2005) I want to be able to roll on the grass in the park, walk and run on the beach and bike ride with her for many years, without her having to give 'Nonna' mouth-to-mouth resuscitation. It's working too....I've lost more weight this past year than ever before and it's staying off.

ANOTHER SOBA NOODLE TALE.......

One of our most devoted food fanatics is a psychologist. You'll see why shortly it's important to know that fact.

She stopped by on her way home one evening, to pick up some dinner. As I was packing her soba noodles to go, we talked non-stop on politics, movies and how teenage years are as much fun as having your teeth pulled. (She has two girls).

We hugged good-bye, and ten minutes later, the phone rang. "Dolores, I think you might have made a mistake and charged me too much." I looked at the sales slip and replied, "Well, let's see. You had 1 1/2 pounds of Soba." There was silence. "Debra, are you there?" No reply. "Debra, are you alright?" No reply. I was getting worried when I heard her barely audible voice say, "Oh my God, the container is almost empty and I'm not even close to my house".

"I need help" she said...maybe I should go into therapy..."No" I replied, "these noodles are so easy to eat because they go down so quickly" ...but the thought of all of those soba noodles disappearing so quickly haunted her for weeks ...

SPICY SOBA NOODLES

INGREDIENTS:

1 lb. Soba noodles

½ cup balsamic vinegar

1 cup brown sugar

¼ cup rice wine vinegar

1 cup soy sauce

2 tbs. molasses

1½ cup sesame oil

1 cup tahini

1-2 oz. chili oil

4 green onions, finely chopped

DIRECTIONS:

In 4 quarts of boiling water, add soba noodles, bring back to boil and cook 1-3 minutes (al dente) "tender but firm to the bite". Drain and rinse with lots of cold water.

SAUCE:

In a blender, mix vinegars, sugar, soy sauce, molasses, tahini, sesame and chili oils. Blend on high for 2 to 3 minutes until thoroughly blended.

Toss with soba noodles and finely chopped green onions.

Serve chilled.

SERVES 4

Remember pasta is always cooked "al dente", no more, no less.

*This is one of only a few recipes that we didn't invent.
An original from one of our past employees....
Thanks Barbara!!!!!!!!

WHATEVER YOU CAN DO,
OR DREAM YOU CAN DO,
BEGIN IT...
BOLDNESS HAS GENIUS,
POWER AND MAGIC
IN IT

—GOETHE

MATCHMAKER, MATCHMAKER
MAKE ME A.....

My buddy Jerry Pearlman MD, named me The "Godmother" for life. He anointed me with that tag at UCLA. His reasoning seemed simple enough. I had 200 people who, as wild as this sounds, reported directly to me; I am Italian; I yell a lot, and when I do, people seem to listen.

As time went on, I realized that I really had an affinity for working with people. I thoroughly enjoyed being with them most of the time, except when they started whining or asking for something impossible, then I threw them out of my office.

My mother had the same talent, (except she was much more gracious than I and would have never thrown anyone out of anywhere.)

My grandma also brought comfort to her Italian friends who settled on the East Side. Grandma D'Eletto's 'stoop' was always filled with hungry men and women trying to find their way in New York. Maybe it's a gift, or maybe we just can't stay out of other people's lives. I'd like to think that three generations helped rather than meddled in people's lives.

When I was a kid, I always ran home from school to see what was happening in my kitchen each day. My mother was usually sipping coffee, talking to someone about anything and everyone was always eating...It was like a never ending smorgasbord.

In the 50's, nobody got divorced. They just stayed miserable. At least in my neighborhood. "Concentrate on your cooking, and your marriage will emphatically improve,," that was my grandma's solace.

The Godmother of Malibu was an extension of my mother's kitchen. My Mom put people together, turning enemies into friends and friends into lovers....how? By using food as a cure-all for everything.

I love food, too, but, listening, sharing, and matching people gives me so much joy. I need to see how people react when they enjoy a good meal, delicious wine and good conversation. Besides a baby's or a puppy's breath, can you really think of anything better?

My best matchmaking experience happened one Valentine's Day.

Denise di Garmo and her then-husband Barry were Godmother good friends and clients from the first day we opened.

This was critical to our survival at the time. Malibu is a funny place—lots of money around, but it's hard to make a buck. When you're the new kid on the block, you must depend on your day-to-day business. The guy who comes in every morning for a bagel and coffee, or the couple who buy chicken pasta every Friday night, are the regulars who will carry you when a landslide closes the highway. Denise and Barry were those people. Denise was there everyday. Her daughter, Sarah, was attending 'Ballet by the Sea', a distinguished dance studio for young girls and boys, which was three doors down from the shop.

Denise bought cookies, pasta, couscous and other specials for dinner most evenings. Barry, an attorney, needed to entertain frequently, and we were fortunate enough to cater all of their parties.

The one party that made my heart sing was a Valentine's dinner at a beach house in Paradise Cove, a secluded beach community about eight miles from the center of Malibu. Here on a secret beach, away from the crowds and inches from the famous set for *The Rockford Files*, the hit television show starring James Garner, was this beautiful view of all of Malibu, rimmed by the Pacific.

A perfect place for such a dinner.

Let me go back a couple of weeks. Denise and I liked to sit around the shop creating different scenarios. She's a writer, and I'm the Godmother. Is this a blessing or a curse? I loved fixing people's lives, so when she told me she was having Barry Levinson, the famed and very talented film director for Valentine's Day dinner, I suggested that she also invite our customers, Paula Weinstein and her husband,

Mark Rosenberg, both successful producers. Remember, I am a movie fanatic. Barry Levinson's movie *Diner* was one of my all-time favorites, *The Natural*, a baseball classic, *Rain Man* the list goes on and on of great movies. Paula and Mark also produced some terrific films. *Something to Talk About*, *The Fabulous Baker Boys*, *American Flyers*...... I felt so strongly that if they could meet, nothing but sheer movie-making history would occur.

Denise, who was crazy enough to listen, jumped at the idea, and because she knew all of the players, set the stage for what was about to be not only a night of romance, but one of the most important meetings of talent in the film industry.

Prior to the party, we had a week of Santa Ana winds, which always makes people a little batty, (and scared for fear of fire) but the wind stopped blowing on Valentine's Day (another Angel?). On this night, the stars were bright, and there was an extraordinary bright yellow full moon. The waves created the music for the scene. It all seemed so consummate.

We were scared. What if they took an instant dislike to each other? But my intuition is rarely wrong, and I knew from their visits to the shop, that neither Paula nor Mark had overgrown egos. Denise said the same for Barry. You can tell a great deal about people from their body of work and all of them have done such creative stuff. I was optimistic.

Marlys and I decided to go for broke. We created a feast of hearts: heart-shaped coconut shrimp, zucchini pie with heart kisses, eggplant salad in heart tins. Dessert was heart-shaped chocolate truffle cakes. When they toasted with champagne in flutes that were decorated with hearts, I knew that a promise of a relationship was bound to happen. Barry Levison and Paula Weinstein went on to produce some wonderful movies together, like *Bandits*, *The Perfect Storm* and *Analyze This...and That*.

Barry Levinson and Paula Weinstien became one of the most successful movie-making teams in the industry and I liked to think that Denise and I had a trifle to do with creating that perfect pairing....

SPINACH PIE

INGREDIENTS:

2 ½ cups ricotta cheese

3 large eggs, broken

½ cup Parmesan cheese

¼ tsp. nutmeg, freshly ground

1 medium onion, finely diced

12 oz. frozen spinach, thawed and drained

6 sheets phyllo dough, thawed

¼ cup butter, melted

DIRECTIONS:

Preheat oven to 375^0.

Spray an 8x8 baking dish with vegetable spray or brush with canola oil.

In a medium bowl, add 3 eggs, ricotta cheese, parmesan cheese and nutmeg. Blend well. Take thawed and drained spinach in small batches, squeeze out all excessive water. Add spinach to ricotta mixture.

Sauté chopped onions in 2 teaspoons of melted butter until soft and clear. Place in the bowl with ricotta and spinach. Mix well and set aside.

Brush 4 sheets of phyllo dough with butter, placing each sheet on top of each other in the bottom of the 8x8 pan. Pour spinach mixture into pan on top of phyllo dough, push into corners so top is even. Fold edges of phyllo dough over top of spinach mixture.

SPINACH PIE
(CONTINUED)

Brush 2 remaining phyllo sheets with butter, fold in half, place on top of spinach pie and tuck in edges of baking dish. Brush remaining butter on top of phyllo dough.

Bake in 375⁰ oven 30 to 40 minutes, till golden brown.

Pure perfection if served with a chilled Greek salad.

Serves 4

VEGETABLE BIRYANI

INGREDIENTS:

1 ½ cups basmatic rice

3 ½ cups chicken broth

1 pinch saffron

1 tsp. tumeric

2 tbs. butter, sweet and melted

1 cup onion, finely chopped

2 tbs. ginger, grated

1 tbs. cumin, toasted

1 tsp. coriander

1 tsp. cinnamon

1 pinch cayenne

1 medium carrot, peeled and shredded

2 cups cauliflower floweretts

1 medium red bell pepper, chopped

1 cup frozen peas

¾ cup golden raisins

¾ cup cashews or almonds, toasted

DIRECTIONS:

Heat oven to 375⁰. Bring chicken broth to a boil.

In a large frying pan, melt butter. Add onion, ginger, cumin, coriander, cinnamon, cayenne, carrots, bell pepper and cauliflower floweretts. Sauté 10 minutes.

VEGETABLE BIRYANI
(CONTINUED)

In a 3-quart baking dish, add the basmati rice, the sautéed vegetables, raisins, chick peas and the boiling chicken broth. Cover with foil.

Place in a 375^0 oven for 30 to 40 minutes, till broth is absorbed.

Removed from oven to a warm place; keep covered for 10 minutes.

Place frozen grean peas in microwave for 3 minutes.

Stir green peas into biryani, fluff with a fork, top with toasted cashews or almonds and serve.

Serve with anything!, roasted chicken, honey baked chicken, fish, grilled vegetables.

Serves 6

BUTTERMILK WHITE CAKE

INGREDIENTS:

5 egg whites

½ lb. sweet butter, softened

2 cups white sugar

1 ½ tsp. vanilla

4 cups cake flour, sifted

2 tsp. baking powder, sifted

1 ½ tsp. baking soda, sifted

1 tsp. Godmother salt

2 cups buttermilk

5 medium egg yolks beaten

DIRECTIONS:

Heat oven to 350°.

Beat 5 egg whites on high till they form stiff peaks; set aside.

In a large mixing bowl, cream together ½ pound softened butter and 2 cups sweetened butter till smooth, then add vanilla.

Sift together all dry ingredients.

Alternate dry ingredients and buttermilk, then add egg yolks, mix till well blended.

Pour cake mix into well greased and floured pan.

Bake at 350° degrees for 25 to 35 minutes, depending on size of pan.

MUSIC IS BREATHING
MUSIC IS SADNESS
MUSIC IS ABOUT LOVE
MUSIC IS LIFE

—PETER MATZ
NOTED MUSICAL ARRANGER

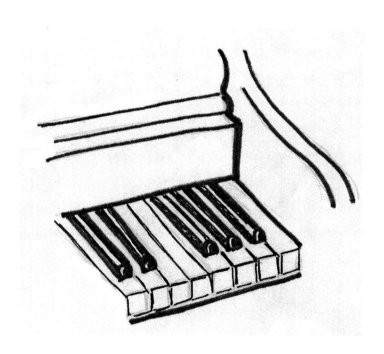

CYMBALIC EVENT

In an age of disposable everything, it is amazing that a 300-year old business actually still exists and in Los Angeles no less.

Nothing has been in Los Angeles 300 years except sunshine and earthquakes. In fact this company is the oldest-run family company in the world, which started in Turkey in 1623, when a sultan who named the company Zildjian (which means "cymbalsmith") discovered a secret metallurgical formula. Since then Zildjian carved a reputation for the finest cymbal craftsmanship with most of the musical world's greats, from Bach to the Beatles; from Jefferson Airplane to Pat Benetar and Neal Giraldo.

To celebrate the opening of their first Los Angeles showroom they put on a feast of mouth-watering Godmother specialities.

On my long list of "Things to do before I leave this earth", kept in the back of my Filofax, is "learn to play drums." So this event was a thrill for me, like an E ticket at Disneyland (when E tickets were the best ride you could get). And what a ride this was. Fifteen hundred musicians and friends were invited from all over the world, and unlike most Los Angeles events, everyone showed up.

From classical to hard rock, they all shared hearty appetites. There is no one word to describe the evening: It was brilliant, glorious, splendid, topped by magnificent. One musician after another entertained in between the appetizers. I could barely concentrate on the food service, I was so mesmerized by the talent.

In July, 2000, we had the pleasure of catering the wedding reception for Michael Zildjian at The Serra Retreat in Malibu. It was a another memorable musical moment and the cymbals continue to ring out for The Godmother of Malibu.

I will play those drums some day!!

GODMOTHER'S HOT MAMMA PIA's PEPPERS

INGREDIENTS:

1 32-oz. jar hot cherry peppers

12 oz. seasoned bread crumbs

¼ cup pine nuts

1 tsp. garlic, minced

¼ cup parmesan cheese, grated

1 ½ tbs. honey

¼ tsp. oregano

¼ tsp. basil

¼ cup chopped parsley

¼ cup imported provolone cheese, grated

4 tbs. olive oil

½ cup premium red wine

DIRECTIONS:

Preheat oven to 375⁰.

Drain hot cherry peppers, cut off tops and scoop out seeds; set aside.

In a medium bowl, add the seasoned bread crumbs, pine nuts, minced garlic, and grated parmesan cheese. Drizzle on honey, oregano, basil, chopped parsley and grated provolone cheese. Toss all ingredients until well-blended. Add 4 tablespoons of olive oil and blend well.

Stuff each cherry pepper and set on a cookie sheet.

Sprinkle cherry peppers with red wine.

GODMOTHER'S HOT
MAMMA PIA's PEPPERS
(CONTINUED)

Place in 375° degree oven, uncovered.

Bake for 20 minutes.

Serve warm or at room temperature.

DEVILED EGGS

INGREDIENTS:

6 hard boiled eggs

1 tsp. sour cream

½ tsp. wasabi powder

  (or 1" strip of wasabi paste)

½ tsp. Godmother Mediterranean salt

DIRECTIONS:

Cut eggs in half lengthwise and remove yolks.

Place yolks in a sieve and mash with a spoon through the sieve.

Place the mashed yolks in a small bowl and add mayonnaise, sour cream, salt and wasabi.

Mix well with a wire whisk.

Place halved egg whites on a platter and fill with yolk mixture.

Decorate with parsley and cilantro.

Serves 6

MINI POTATOES WITH CAVIAR

INGREDIENTS:

6 baby red potatoes, 2 inches in diameter

1 oz. American caviar

6 oz. sour cream

1/3 cup chives, diced

DIRECTIONS:

Bake baby red potatoes in a 400⁰ oven for 30 to 40 minutes, until tender when a fork is inserted.

Cool potatoes 15 minutes, cut 1 inch 'X' marks in top of potatoes, and squeeze until edges of potatoes rise up. Remove extra potato from center to form a small well.

Fill center of potato with a spoonful of sour cream. For a fancy touch, pipe sour cream with fitted rose bud tip.

Chop 1/3 cup of chives, and save six 1 inch tips for decorating. Sprinkle chopped chives over sour cream.

Divide the 1 ounce of caviar among the six potatoes, placing one little spoonful on top of sour cream.

Take the 1 inch tip of chive and place in sour cream, next to caviar, like a feather.

STUFFED ARTICHOKES

INGREDIENTS:

4 large artichokes

1 large lemon, cut in half

2 quarts water

2 tbs. olive oil

2 cups bread crumbs

¼ cup Parmesan cheese, grated

2 cloves of garlic, minced

1 tsp. fresh oregano, minced

pinch of Godmother salt and some pepper

¼ cup black olives, sliced

2 whole eggs, beaten

¼ cup olive oil,

STUFFING:

Mix together bread crumbs, parmesan cheese, minced garlic, oregano, beaten eggs, olive oil, salt and pepper and sliced olives.

DIRECTIONS:

Cut off both ends of the artichokes. Trim the ends of the leaves off with kitchen scissors. Rub the cut ends with half a lemon to prevent browning.

With a sharp paring knife, cut out the inner leaves, down to the heart. Stuff with bread crumb mixture.

STUFFED ARTICHOKES
(CONTINUED)

Place the four stuffed artichokes in a pan tight enough so that they don't tip over. Add enough water to come half way up the artichoke, Add cut lemons to water, and drizzle the tops of the artichokes with olive oil.

Bring water to a boil, cover, reduce heat to a gentle boil, cook for 1 hour or till outer leaves pull off easily.

SERVES 4

PARMESAN PUFFS

(an original Godmother creation)

INGREDIENTS:

12 ¼" sliced pieces of baguette

¼ cup minced yellow onion

1 cup mayonnaise

2 oz. or ¼ cup swiss cheese, shredded

1 oz. or 1/8 cup parmesan cheese, grated

½ tsp. Worcestershire sauce

DIRECTIONS:

Slice a french or sourdough baguette into 12 ¼ inch slices. Let them dry out at room temperature for 1 to 2 hours.

In a medium mixing bowl, add mayonnaise, minced onion, shredded swiss cheese, grated parmesan cheese and Worcestershire sauce. Mix well.

Place sliced baguettes on a cookie sheet. Top each slice with 1 tablespoon of the cheese mixture.

Place under broiler for 1 to 3 minutes until brown and bubbly.

Appetizer for 4.....

JUST CHARGE IT

A kid walks into the shop one muggy afternoon. He was about eight or nine years old, bony-thin, with long hair covering his eyes. His pants kept falling below his hips, and between trying to hold them up and keep his hair out of his eyes, he was a busy little soul.

Although I was busy with a customer, I felt his presence and cut my conversation short. As I approached him, I thought, "What a good-looking kid that is." He had a dark complexion, sharp, chiseled features, bright eyes (that you could barely see through the hair) and a marvelous smile that took up his entire face. He certainly had a strong presence for a young kid.

Before I could open my mouth, he said, "Hi, can I have a Godmother sandwich?" "Sure," I replied. He asked me what was in it, and he seemed happy when I told him. "That's $5.75," I said as I handed him the wrapped sandwich. Without looking up, he tore at the paper, barely getting his little mouth around the big roll, took a huge bite, and mumbled, "Charge it to my mom," and out the door he ran.

"Hey kid," I yelled, "get back here." He stopped dead in his tracks, still chewing, turned and looked at me with a puzzled expression, like "What's the problem, lady?"

"What's your name, and who's your mother?"

"Oh," he pause, and then said, "Josh, and my mom's Ali MacGraw." No wonder he's so adorable, I thought.

I had never met Ali MacGraw. Obviously at that point, she didn't have a charge account. That didn't matter. I am truly thankful for that encounter with that kid who had no money, but did have the tenacity to walk into our shop for the very first time with a self-assurance most adults spend fortunes in therapy developing. No short talk, no kid talk, he just took control of the situation.

THE GODMOTHER SANDWICH

INGREDIENTS:

6" submarine roll

2 oz. house dressing

3 slices provolone cheese

2 slices mortadella

3 slices ham

8 slices Genoa salami

3 oz. marinated onions

5 slices tomato

DRESSING:

1/3 cup red wine vinegar

2/3 cup extra virgin olive oil

1 tsp. dried basil

1 tsp. dried oregano

1 clove finely chopped garlic

DIRECTIONS:

Cut submarine roll ¾ of the way through.

Brush on a lot of house dressing.

The cold cuts MUST be placed on the rolls as they are listed above—first the cheese, then the mortadella, ham, salami.

Add marinated onions and sliced tomatoes and cut in half.

NEVER USE PACKAGED COLD CUTS

SERVING: 1

MR. MALIBU

Burgess Meredith was a true icon of the film world and the Malibu community. Known for his portrayal of the tough yet loving fight manager in the Rocky movies of the 80's, he was an extraordinary actor who left us with film memories such as *Madam X*, my favorite Lana Turner movie and John Steinbeck's *Of Mice and Men*, in which he played a gut-wrenching George. He appeared in *A Wedding*, Robert Altman's brilliant film, and *True Confessions* opposite Robert De Niro and Robert Duvall. In *Batman* he played "the Penguin." His last films, *Grumpy Old Men* and it's sequel, featured him with the likes of Ann Margaret and Sophia Loren—and he held his own very nicely.

In addition to his talents as an actor, he was also a connoisseur and collector of fine wines, with a side passion for good food.

He had his own small, well-stocked wine cellar flowing with the best and oldest vintages. He was a Godmother regular. We were always delighted to include him on our exclusive client list for Thanksgiving and Christmas catering.

Concerned about Malibu's direction and growth, he opened his home and his pocketbook many times to help support the birth of the city. At one of his huge galas at his beach home for the first city council candidates of the newly formed City of Malibu, hundreds crowded in to hear the candidates extoil their own virtues.

The wines flowed and the candidates did what candidates do— they gave long boring speeches, promising everything to everyone.

Burgess and I shared a rare bottle of wine after the guests left and talked for hours.

"So what do you think of the candidates?" he asked.

"If this is the best we have in Malibu, I think we're in trouble," I replied. (I've worked with all of these people to form the Incorporation Committee.).

Each of these candidates had separate agendas not comparable with the city's needs. In a nutshell, if they were the best, Malibu was in for some rocky moments.

"Although I do believe they are decent, honest and committed Malibuites, I think the power and the glory play too big a part." I said.

Burgess, also known as Mr. Malibu exclaimed, "Now you tell me, after I spent all this money on the party!"

(Note: Despite my skepticism, the first city council members did a very credible job under difficult circumstances. The one glaring problem I saw was that they stayed too long in office).

SKEWERED SHRIMP with BASIL

INGREDIENTS:

12 6" bamboo skewers

24 medium shrimp, raw with tails

24 large basil leaves

¾ cup olive oil

¼ cup lemon juice

1 tsp. crushed red peppers

1 tsp. garlic, minced

DIRECTIONS:

Soak 12 6" bamboo skewers in warm water for 1 hour (this prevents skewers from burning while grilling).

Remove shells from shrimp, leaving tails in place. Run paring knife down top side of shrimp to remove vein. Rinse and pat dry.

Wrap basil leaf around shrimp. Run skewer through shrimp and basil twice to hold in place (shrimp will form a "C"). Place two shrimp with basil on each 6" skewer.

In a small bowl, mix 1 teaspoon of minced garlic, 1 teaspoon of crushed red peppers, ¾ cup of olive oil, ¼ cup of lemon juice. Whisk until all ingredients are well blended.

Brush shrimp skewers with olive oil-lemon juice mixture.

Grill over hot coals, brushing with olive oil mixture frequently. Grill 2 to 3 minutes on each side, until shrimp is pink and opaque.

NOTE: Shrimp is cooked when it is pink and opaque, and forms a relaxed C. Shrimp is overcooked when it forms an "O", or when the tail touches the head end.

FLUFFY RICE

1 cup converted white rice, rinsed

2 cups chicken stock, salted to taste

½ cup parsley, chopped

DIRECTIONS:

Spray a 1 quart baking dish with vegetable spray or grease with olive oil.

Preheat oven to 400⁰.

Add the rinsed white rice and chicken stock to baking dish. Cover with foil.

Bake at 400⁰, covered, for 30 – 40 minutes. Uncover, let stand for 15 minutes.

Fluff with a fork, adding the chopped parsley until well mixed.

Serve warm or at room temperature.

*Great served with Dixie's Curried Chicken Salad.

Serves 4

SALMON TARTARE

INGREDIENTS:

2 salmon, boneless and skinless

1 medium red onion, finely sliced

3 tbs. dill, chopped fine

2 tbs. capers, drained

1 tsp. lemon juice

2 tbs. olive oil

3 tbs. acquavit

Godmother salt and some pepper to taste

DIRECTIONS:

In a food processor or by hand, finely chop salmon, being careful not to puree it. Hand chopping, over and over until a fine minced salmon is achieved gives the best texture.

In a medium bowl, place minced salmon, finely diced red onions, minced dill and capers. Toss with lemon juice, olive oil and acquavit. Salt and pepper to taste. Chill at least 2 hours.

Serve on thin Swedish crackers or pumpernickel rounds, with dill sauce.

Makes 12 portions

THE GODMOTHER'S KALUA PORK

INGREDIENTS:

2 5 lbs. pork butts, cut into 3 or 4 pieces

3 tbs. Godmother salt

1 tsp. liquid smoke

DIRECTIONS:

In a large pan cover pork butts with cold water. Add salt and liquid smoke. Cover pan with parchment paper and foil.

Cook 375^0 for 3 hours.

Remove from oven and cool for approximately 1 hour. Shred pork and cover with cooking liquid. Place in refrigerator and chill overnight. In am, drain liquid.

KALUA PORK SAUCE

INGREDIENTS:

8 cups BBQ sauce

2 onions diced fine and grilled

1 cup apple cider vinegar

1 cup brown sugar

3 tbs. Worchester sauce

½ cup dijon mustard

1 tsp. Godmother salt

4 tbs. lemon juice

DIRECTIONS:

Add all ingredients into 4-quart sauce pan. Simmer on low for 1 hour, stirring frequently.

To serve, shredded pork, top with Kalua sauce, cover and heat in 325° oven for 20 minutes.

NOW THIS IS POT ROAST

INGREDIENTS:

4-5 lbs. tri-tip roast

Lots of garlic (at least ½ cup chopped)

1 cup extra virgin olive oil

4 chopped carrots

8 stalks celery chopped

2 large onions diced

2 cups dry red wine

3 tbs. thyme

2 bay leaves

3 tbs. Godmother salt

DIRECTIONS:

Heat ollive oil in a heavy pan, add meat and garlic, brown on both sides

Add carrots, celery and onions to pot.

Let brown some more

Then add wine, thyme, salt, bay leaves and enough water to cover meat and vegetables

Simmer on top of stove 3 to 4 hours. Add more water if needed.

8 servings

THAT-A – LIST

One of the most beautiful and elegant actresses I have ever met asked us to handle her mother's notable- age birthday party at a Malibu Colony beach house she was renting for the summer.

Trust me, this woman is a first class ticket anywhere. She exudes style and taste, and for this event, she requested some very special china, silver and crystal that most rental companies do not have in stock.

I turned to Billie Gay for help. As a poor kid growing up in the South, Billie Gay decided she was never going to do without.

She had huge storage cabinets at her home, filled with everything we could possibly want, and then some. She bought silver, china and crystal just for the fun of owning such elegant stuff. I bet Tiffany's didn't have an inventory like hers.

When she died, her husband Bill asked me to help him return these lovely items because, he thought they were borrowed. I looked at his sad face and said, "You own it all!"

How many people know someone who wraps silver utensils in wax paper and secures it with rubber bands?..., I've had the distinction of knowing two such characters. The first one was the mother of my grade school pal, and the other was Billie Gay. These two people were as different as a nun and a stripper. Well, maybe nuns and strippers are closer than we think, but these two at least were polar opposites.

My friends mother was anal retentive and controlling. Billie Gay was carefree and loved the challenge of chaos. She thought nothing of lending her $55,000 Lincoln Contenental Mark V automobile (a fortune in 1980's) to anyone who asked. If it came back damaged, she merely behaved very Southern (sweetly graceful).

Yet she treated her 1847 Roger's Brothers silver service utensils as though they were part of the crown jewels of England.

She could have opened a rental company....She had everything I needed for this event silver, crystal, gold-edged dishes and linens.

The actress requested that we arrive thirty minutes before the guests were due.

"We need much more time I said" I wasn't about to share with her the unwrapping adventure with each fork, knife and spoon in addition to the normal time it takes to set up the kitchen, the food stations and the bar, but she seemed determined to keep us away from the house until the very last minute...

As a pretty perceptive person, she immediately realized my stress level was rising, so we compromised.

Set-up began one and a half hours before the guests were scheduled to arrive. Not a great deal of time but I felt if we hustled, we could get it done ... Wrong!!! A half-hour into the set-up, I heard music and its coming from the front of the house. I ran to the front window, and yelled "F...". I saw a huge orchestra (which turned out to be the Los Angeles Philharmonic) led by singer Andy Williams, approaching the house, singing *Happy Birthday*, followed by hoards of people heading towards the front door.

"This is a joke", I said to myself.... We were still unpeeling the wax paper from the silver.

Momentarily stunned, I yelled for our beauty and said, with a smile, "Tell them they have the wrong day."

Her face was frozen. "I was afraid no one would come to my party," she whispered.

"WHAT?" I yelled, and without thinking, I grabbed her arm and practically dragged her into the bathroom near the kitchen.

"Look in the mirror," I said, "Everyone and anyone would show up for you, and they just did." The room was so tiny that we stood shoulder to shoulder. Her face was ashen...she felt my pain.

I ran from the bathroom to the kitchen and started practically slingling appetizers to the crowds that were piling through the house.

Our beauty spent the entire afternoon apologizing to her guests, because we weren't ready and explaining that it was her misunderstanding about the 'time'. She also apologized to me. But I didn't want an apology—she did nothing wrong. I understood what she was feeling. Everyone feels anxious when they give a party. If the guests arrive before you expect them, most hostesses want to cut their wrists...Our job is to create an atmosphere of peace and serenity so they can enjoy their own party and remove that awful feeling of stress.

Food therapy it's called.

Hollywood is a brutal scene. Many a beautiful face has been smashed on the bathroom floor over such trivia. She was not a mega star at that time, but she was high on that list, so called the Hollwood "A" list. Ironically, she became a mega star years later.

I hope she never worried again about anyone showing up.

She is a very special lady and I always think of her with sincere affection.

GRILLED EGGPLANT & GOAT CHEESE ROLLS

INGREDIENTS:

½ cup olive oil

1 large eggplant

½ cup ricotta cheese

3 ounces goat cheese

1 tsp. garlic, minced

2 tbs. fresh basil, minced

1 ½ tbs. balsamic vinegar

DIRECTIONS:

Cut eggplant lengthwise into 12 or 14 1/8 inch slices. Brush both sides of eggplant slices with olive oil and grill on hot griddle or large fry pan until deep brown. Let cool.

In a medium mixing bowl, add ½ cup ricotta cheese, 2 ounces of goat cheese, 1 teaspoon of minced garlic, 2 tablespoons of fresh, minced basil, and mix all the ingredients well with a fork.

Lay out grilled eggplant slices and place 2 tablespoons of the cheese-basil mixture on bottom edge. Roll up all the way to the top.

Sprinkle eggplant rolls with balsamic vinegar.

Serve chilled or at room temperature.

Makes 12.

GODMOTHER PATÉ

INGREDIENTS:

1 cup butter

½ cup chopped onion

¼ cup chopped, peeled apple

2 tbs. chopped shallots

1 lb. chicken livers

¼ cup brandy

2-3 tbs. whipping cream

1 tsp. lemon juice

1 tsp. Godmother salt

¼ tsp. black pepper

½ cup clarified butter (optional)

DIRECTIONS:

Soften 10 tablespoons butter and set aside.

Melt 3 tablespoons of butter in skillet. Add onions and shallots. Cook, stirring, until tender, about 5 minutes.

Add apple, and cook until tender, about 3 minutes. Place apple mixture in blender container.

Melt another 3 tablespoons butter in skillet. Add chicken livers and stir 3 to 4 minutes until livers are browned outside and pink inside.

Add brandy and stir 2 minutes longer.

Add liver mixture to blender container.

Add 2 tablespoons cream and blend until smooth at high speed.

Add more cream, if necessary, to keep mixture smooth.

GODMOTHER PATÉ
(CONTINUED)

Press through medium fine strainer into mixing bowl.

Cool thoroughly, stirring once or twice. (Paté will become oily if not completely cooled).

Cream softened 10 tablespoons of butter in mixer and add liver mixture, a little at a time, beating well after each addition.

Pour paté into crock or ramekins, smoothing top with spatula.

Pour enough clarified butter over top to form seal (optional).

CAPELLI D'ANGELO GODMOTHER

INGREDIENTS:

1 lb. capellini pasta

3 green onions, sliced

1 medium red bell pepper, seeded and diced

4 oz. gorgonzola cheese, crumbled

½ cup olive oil

2 tbs. red wine vinegar

1/8 tsp. oregano

1 pinch Godmother salt and some pepper

4 oz. jar marinated artichokes, chopped

4 stalks hearts of palm, chopped

2 tbs. parsley, minced

DIRECTIONS:

Add 1 pound of capellini to 8 quarts of boiling, salted water. Cook (al dente) "tender but firm to the bite", 6 to 8 minutes. Drain and rinse 2 or 3 times in cool water.

Place cooked, drained pasta in a medium bowl. Add the sliced green onion, diced red bell pepper, and 3 ounces of the crumbled gorgonzola cheese to the pasta, and toss until well blended.

In a blender, pour the olive oil, red wine vinegar, 1 ounce of gorgonzola, oregano, salt and pepper, and blend until smooth. Pour dressing over pasta and toss until well coated. Place in a serving bowl.

Drain marinated artichokes, and save the marinade in a small bowl. Chop artichokes and add them to the marinade.

CAPELLI D'ANGELO GODMOTHER
(CONTINUED)

Slice hearts of palm in small round pieces, and add to the artichoke marinade, along with chopped parsley. Toss hearts of palm and artichokes until well marinated.

Place mixture on top of pasta. Chill 1 to 2 hours before serving.

Garnish top of pasta with julienned red pepper.

Serves 6

WILD RICE SALAD

INGREDIENTS:

2 cups water

½ cup wild rice

½ cup barley

¼ cup Thompson seedless raisins

¼ cup golden raisins

½ cup walnuts, coarsely chopped

4 green onions, chopped

1 orange, navel (seedless)

½ cup parsley leaves

1 cup mint leaves

6 oz. vegetable oil

2 oz. lemon juice

DIRECTIONS:

Place ½ cup of wild rice and ½ cup of barley into 2 cups of boiling water. Cover pot and simmer for 40 minutes. Remove from heat and cool.

In a medium bowl, combine cooled rice and barley, black and golden raisins, coarsely chopped walnuts and 4 chopped green onions.

In a food processor with a metal chopping blade, place 1 quartered orange (skin and all) and chop fine.

Add mint leaves, parsley leaves and lemon juice to chopped orange in food processor. With processor running, slowly add vegetable oil to mixture until well blended.

WILD RICE SALAD
(CONTINUED)

Pour orange/mint dressing over rice mixture and toss until well coated. Chill several hours and serve.

Serves 4 - 6

OUR CHOCOLATE "MOUSSE"
With Chopped Toasted Hazelnuts

INGREDIENTS:

12 oz. semi sweet chocolate chips

1 stick unsalted butter

4 eggs separated

2 tbs. sugar

1 cup whipping cream

1 tsp. vanilla extract

1 pinch of Godmother salt

1 tsp. of arrowroot

1 box of raspberries

Handful of toasted hazelnuts

DIRECTIONS:

Melt butter, salt, and chocolate chips for 2 minutes in microwave, stir till smooth.

Beat egg yolks, add to chocolate and combine thoroughly. Set aside to cool

Beat whites with arrowroot, add sugar a little at a time until ingredients form stiff peaks. Fold into chocolate mixture

Beat whipping cream with vanilla until stiff and fold into chocolate mixture.

Chill until firm.

Sprinkle with toasted hazelnuts—garnish with whipped cream and raspberries.

10 servings.

RING AROUND A TAPAS WEDDING

Actor Tom Skerritt (*Mash, A River Runs Through, Alien, Top Gun, The Turning Point, Ice Castles* and many more) and his family were very supportive of our efforts to bring quality food to Malibu. From our very first day, they were "regulars." Tom shared an old family recipe with us for a delicious chocolate fudge sauce that we sold at the shop.

Unfortunately we did not have the capabilities to handle the volume that the fudge sauce demanded at that time. Too bad because it was so delicious. A perfect blend of chocolates and caramel.

When his lovely daughter Erin decided to marry, we were presented with a real challenge. The bride and groom wanted a tapas buffet, which is the customary wedding food in Argentina where the groom was born and raised. The Skerritts wanted an American- style barbecue. The key was to combine both South and North American cultures and deliver a wedding feast for 250 guests.

South American tapas are small portions of foods served from among many selections. Usually, tapas are served as an early evening or late night snack, but for this day they were served as the highlight for a wedding feast. The choices were many and varied. —chicken, beef, fish, vegetables, pastas, rice, beans, potatoes, cheeses ...

For the American barbeque, we offered pork and beef ribs, hot dogs, hamburgers along with baby corn and grilled vegetables for appetizers, which we served on the lawn of the lovely Malibu Lake Country Club.

When dinner was ready, we opened the french doors to the dining room where an oval buffet almost thirty feet in length sat with forty-six different selections of tapas....

Some of the guests had apparently thought the barbecue WAS DINNER and ate a lot. Stuffed and moaning that they could not eat another bite, they moved into the dining room and consumed the entire feast in record time.

This wedding was a record breaker. In twenty-seven plus years and over four hundred weddings, it still ranks as the largest presentation of foods ever offered... two hundred-seventy-three guests were served that day. Would you believe that twenty-three of them were late walk-ins. I was stunned. My first and last 'stunned' about lack of RSVP's. I have since learned that in Los Angeles, RSVPs apparently are just suggestions— so often it's a toss up to determine whose coming to your wedding.

For this particular wedding the late arrivals told us that they just assumed that the Skerritt's knew they were coming. Of course we had enough food, (there was enough food for a Roman legion) but the seating posed a logistical nightmare.

Ironically, despite the elegance of the tapas and its aesthetic ritual, there is a measure of indifference to both table and seating arrangements and even to the food itself, which, although delicate and tasty, can be eaten standing up. Conversation plays an important part of this ritual.

So I was banking on everyone there remembering this sacrosanct tradition and not panicing while we did some very creative adjustments. We played musical chairs.

As guests moved to the buffet table, mulling over their choices (fortunately, it took time because there were so many selections), we moved the late arrivals into seats. It was like a Circle Line Boat tour with 'tour directors' at both ends.

When some guests went to the buffet, the others were returning, and the circle went round and round.

The Angels were definitely watching over us that day. It was a masterful job of combining tradition with reality, and a bit of psychology thrown in too. The late arrivals felt, to their credit, somewhat guilty, so there was not a word of complaint out of their mouths as I moved them around like chess pieces.

On the following page are some of tapas served at the Skerritt wedding.

MARYLAND CRAB CAKES

INGREDIENTS:

1 lb. crab meat

1 cup seasoned bread crumbs

2 eggs

3 tbs. cream

1 small yellow onion, diced

1 green onion, diced

2 stalks celery, finely diced

1 small green bell pepper, diced

1 tsp. dry mustard

½ tsp. cayenne pepper

¼ cup mayonnaise

¼ cup butter, melted

1 cup masa harina (finely ground corn flour)

CORN SALSA:

2 ears of yellow or white corn

4 Roma tomatoes

1 medium red onion, diced

½ cup chopped cilantro leaves

1 small jalapeno pepper, diced

½ cup prepared salsa

MARYLAND CRAB CAKES
(CONTINUED)

Remove kernels of corn from cob with a sharp knife. Place kernels in a bowl cover with damp paper towel. Place in microwave on Hi for 3 minutes. Remove paper towel and cook.

When corn kernels are cool, toss with diced Roma tomatoes, diced red onion, chopped cilantro, chopped jalapeno and salsa. Mix well and serve.

DIRECTIONS:

In a medium bowl, add bread crumbs, eggs, cream, mayonnaise, melted butter, dry mustard and cayenne. Mix well.

Add to bread crumb mixture the diced yellow and green onions, diced celery, diced green bell pepper and crab meat. Mix well.

Shape crab cake mixture into 12 patties and roll in masa harina or bread crumbs. Set on waxpaper covering a cookie sheet, and chill for 30 minutes.

In a medium skillet, add and heat about ½ inch of peanut or corn oil. When oil reaches 375° degrees, fry crab cakes for 3 to 4 minutes on each side, or until golden. Keep finished cakes warm in oven until all batches are done.

SERVES 12

LINGUINI WITH FRESH CLAMS

INGREDIENTS:

12 oz. linguini

4 lbs. of New Zealand green lip clams

3 leeks, white part only

1 bulb of garlic, peeled and chopped

¾ cups of olive oil

1 cup clam juice or chicken stock

1 tsp. Godmother salt

2 tsp. dried oregano

½ tsp. red pepper flakes

DIRECTIONS:

Fill a 4 quart sauce pan ¾ water add a pinch of Godmother salt

Bring to a boil

Wash and scrub clams in cold water. Drain in colander.

Cut leeks in half lengthwise, rinse well and pat dry. Then cut leeks crosswise in ¼ half rounds

Add linguini to boiling water. Cook until (al dente) "tender but firm to the bite" 8 to 10 minutes.

Drain and keep warm.

In a large frying pan, add olive oil and heat 1 to 2 minutes over medium heat. Stir in leeks, garlic and Godmother salt, cook until transparent.

Add 1 cup of clam juice or chicken stock

LINGUINI WITH FRESH CLAMS
(CONTINUED)

Bring to a boil, toss in the oregano and all of the clams. Cover and steam about 3 minutes.

Uncover and remove opened clams to a serving bowl. Continue to remove clams as they open. Discard any unopened clams.

Add the drained pasta and red pepper flakes to the clam sauce. Toss in sauce under medium heat till hot and well coated.

Pour pasta onto serving platter, top with clams and served with freshly grated parmesan cheese.

Serves 4

CHICKEN CACCIATORE

INGREDIENTS:

3 lbs. chicken, cut into pieces*

¾ cup flour

pinch of Godmother salt and some pepper to taste

¼ cup olive oil

¼ cup canola oil

4 cloves garlic, chopped

2 small onions, quartered

1 small green bell pepper, seeded and chopped

1 small red bell pepper, seeded and chopped

16 medium mushrooms, quartered

8 oz. jar marinated artichokes, quartered

1 cup Chianti, for deglazing

16 oz. marinara sauce

2 tbs. brown sugar

1 tsp. oregano

1 tsp. sage, crumbled

DIRECTIONS:

In a large, deep frying pan, heat the olive and canola oil.

Place the flour, salt and pepper in a large plastic bag and dredge half of the chicken pieces and add to the heated oil. Dredge the remaining pieces of chicken and add to the oil. Fry the chicken pieces until they are golden brown on all sides.

CHICKEN CACCIATORE
(CONTINUED)

Remove chicken to a platter and drain the oil from the frying pan. Return frying pan to medium heat and add Chianti wine. Deglaze for 3 minutes.**

Add to the frying pan the marinara sauce, brown sugar, oregano, sage, salt and pepper, and bring to a boil, stirring frequently.

Add the chopped garlic, onions, bell peppers, mushrooms, artichoke hearts, and browned chicken. Bring mixture to a boil. Lower heat to a medium simmer, and cover, stirring every 20 minutes.

Cook for 60 to 95 minutes, until all is tender.

Serves 6

* Always use either range-free or organic chickens — worth the extra cost.

**Deglazing is adding liquid to a pan in which you just sautéd meat or chicken. The idea is to loosen up any bits that have stuck to the pan.

SAUTEED CHICKEN BREAST W/DUXELLE, FONTINA CHEESE

INGREDIENTS:

4 half chicken breasts, skinless and boneless, pat dry
¼ cup flour
½ cup canola or olive oil
Godmother salt and some pepper to taste
1 ½ cups mushrooms, Cuisinart
2 medium shallots, finely chopped
2 tbs. butter, melted
2 tbs. dry sherry
4 slices fontina cheese

DIRECTIONS:

Duxelle Mixture:

In a food processor, finely chop mushrooms. Add the finely chopped mushrooms and finely diced shallots to the 2 tablespoons of melted butter in a medium frying pan. Sauté mushrooms over medium heat until most of liquid is absorbed. Add dry sherry and continue to cook till mixture is dry. Set aside.

Dredge boneless, skinless chicken breast in flour. Heat canola/olive oil in a fry pan, then add chicken breast, salt and pepper, cook on each side till a light golden brown, about 4 minutes on each side.

Remove chicken breast to a baking dish, divide mushroom mixture (duxelle) among the four breasts. Place duxelles on top of each breast, top with a slice of fontina cheese.

Bake uncovered at 375⁰ for 15 minutes.

Serve with a Jasmine coconut mint rice.

Serves 4

BONELESS LEG OF LAMB

INGREDIENTS:

½ cup olive oil

8 cloves garlic, finely chopped

1 tbs. fresh rosemary, finely chopped

1 medium lemon, juiced

1 tbs. kosher salt and some Godmother salt

2 cups good quality red wine

4 tbs. butter, melted

4 tbs. flour

2 cups lamb drippings and stock

DIRECTIONS:

Have your butcher bone the leg of lamb and tie.

Preheat oven to 450°.

Mix together olive oil, juice of 1 lemon, minced rosemary, chopped garlic and salts. Rub the mixture all over leg of lamb. Place the uncovered lamb into a 450° oven for 20 minutes. Baste with red wine.

Reduce heat to 350°, baste every 20 minutes with red wine.

Cook about 20 minutes a pound, until meat thermometer reaches desired temperature and doneness.

Rare —> 140-145; medium 145-160, well done 160-170. Set aside, cover with foil, let rest 15 minutes before carving.

Add stocked or water to meat drippings to make 4 cups.

BONELESS LEG OF LAMB
(CONTINUED)

In a medium saucepan, melt 4 tablespoons butter, whisk in flour, let it bubble (or cook 3 minutes), whisk in lamb drippings and ½ cup red wine. Salt and pepper to taste, stirring frequently until thick.

Serve with garlic mashed potatoes and steamed spinach.

Serves 4

MS. TRUDI'S "GOD"ZILLA SHRIMP

INGREDIENTS:

1 lb. colossal (8-12 count) raw shrimp (shells on preferably)

2 cups dry white wine

1/8 cup finely chopped shallots

2 tbs. canola oil

2 tbs. butter

2 tbs. garlic, chopped

6 cloves

Godmother salt & white pepper to taste

3 tbs. cold unsalted butter

2 tbs. fresh thyme leaves

2 tbs. finely chopped parsley

½ cup chopped tomatoes

DIRECTIONS:

Remove shells from shrimp leaving tails on reserving the shells. Bring wine, shells, chopped shallots and 3 branches of fresh thyme to a boil, then lower to medium heat. Remove contents and save liquid. Put cold butter into liquid and whisk until mixture is slightly thickened. Set aside.

Heat sauté pan over high heat, add oil and shrimp (do not crowd them) cook about 1 minute add cloves, chopped tomatoes, and liquid, cook another minute. Salt and pepper to taste, sprinkle with chopped Italian parsley and fresh thyme.

Serves 4-6

"ROCKIN" WITH THE TRUTH

The business manager for a very talented rock-star wanted to throw a birthday surprise party for his client at his Hollywood hills home and although I'm not much of a rock-and-roller, I liked this guy's music very much.

I arrived at this attractive yet surprisingly unpretentious home in the hills above Hollywood and the butler (that's what the manager called him even though he was dressed in torn shorts and a rock t-shirt) led me into the master bedroom. I was not happy with our meeting location but nothing surprises me in Hollywood, anymore. Entering the room, I was somewhat amused. The guy I was meeting was lying in bed, dressed in bright yellow silk pajamas, his Jack Russell terrier in his arms, leaning against the largest pillows I've ever seen...talking on the phone.

He was so huge that the pajamas he was wearing looked like the bed spread...I couldn't see where the pajamas ended and the sheets began.

He was surrounded by those things that I guess makes one feel important—pedigree dog, phones, scripts!!!

Along the walls were two computers, three televisions, several Grammy's, and loads of stereo equipment. I wasn't impressed. I'm from New York remember, and so very jaded when it comes to material acquisitions.

A hundred guests were expected and since this wasn't a very big house, it was obvious that we would need to cover the pool to accommodate dinner tables. "I'm paying the tab" was the first sentence out of his mouth. I want to keep the costs reasonable". Oh, what a surprise, I thought.

It was a long and very tiresome meeting. He kept insisting on quantities of food that wouldn't have fed a bunch of blue jay's. After an hour or so, I was getting bored and tired of repeating, "You must have enough food for one hundred guests". But he kept 'chewing on the nickel' (my own 'expression' for being cheap) so I made a mental note to insure enough food and took off.

I only agreed to meet with this guy and do this party as a favor to the rock star's attorney and his wife, who were long time customers and friends.

On party day, the arriving guests were greeted with loud, rock music, appetizers and iced cold drinks to whet their appetites. The evening was most enjoyable, and people were relaxing after dinner, enjoying the cool summer evening, waiting for dessert.

The kitchen was tiny and crowded with staff trying to plate up the dessert. I heard the birthday boy's voice behind me. "When will the main course be served?" he asked. "You've had the main course", I said "We will be serving dessert next."

A strange look crossed his face, but he said nothing except "thank you" and left. I peeked around the corner and saw him approach his manager, who was standing at the staircase saying goodbye to a few guests. I could barely hear what the rock star was saying, but clearly I heard the manager's words, "Oh God, the caterer forgot the beef and salmon I ordered. I was hoping no one would notice."

"What?" I shouted and ran out of the kitchen. I had to leap up to get past his huge mass of body so that I could grab him by his shirt collar and screamed, "You didn't want to spend any more money, you creep! Tell him the truth!" I let go of his shirt, which now had a few less buttons. He was perspiring and said nothing. The rock star starred at him, and without saying a word, walked away.

If I ever find enough time and energy, I'd like to write two more books … A Godmother trilogy … book two, on weddings/marriage, and book three on money … very, very sensitive subject and one of life's biggest lessons.

Oh, do I have a whole lot of opinion here, but in fairness to you, the reader who probably was just looking for a cookbook, and got a trifle more, I'm saving my philosophies on life for the "trilogy". You never know... if I ever head to that patch of sand on Kauai or that farm house in Umbria, it's possible. But I will leave you with one little bitsy bit of Godmother wisdom.

The only thing money could possibly bring into your life is freedom. Doesn't guarantee you another thing, not another day on this Earth, not a prime parking space in the middle of Beverly Hills, not the ability to lose ten pounds overnight to fit into your wedding dress, not a report card from your kids sporting all A's... not a full house at poker ... nothing ... nothing at all ... just one thing ... FREEDOM.

Considering the history with this cookbook, it could be decades before any other book saw the light of day, so take these bits of wisdom now. If you have a few extra bucks someday, trying sharing with someone less fortunate. The gifts you will receive in return, will be priceless.

SANTA FE SALAD

INGREDIENTS:

4 chicken breast halves without skin

½ cup olive oil, whisked

2 tbs. lemon juice

1 tsp. garlic, minced

2 tbs. cumin

1 large red bell pepper, cut into 1" triangles

1 large green bell pepper, cut into 1" triangles

1 medium red onion, 1" pieces

1 cup corn kernels, grilled

1 tbs. parsley, minced

1 tbs. cilantro, minced

1 cup jicama, julienned

12 Kalamata olives

2 medium Roma tomatoes, diced

2 tbs. lemon juice

½ tsp. Tabasco sauce

Godmother salt and some pepper to taste

DIRECTIONS:

Marinate boneless, skinless chicken breast in marinade made of whisked olive oil, lemon juice, garlic and cumin and put in refrigerator for 4 hours. Grill on barbecue or on stove's grill, 4 to 5 minutes each side, let cool.

SANTA FE SALAD
(CONTINUED)

On a flat top or in a skillet, grill bell peppers, onions, and corn kernels. Let cool.

Toss cooled julienned chicken, grilled vegetables, jicama, calamata olives, Roma tomatoes, parsley, and cilantro, with a dressing whisked with olive oil, lemon juice, Tabasco, salt and pepper.

Serve at room temperature or chilled.

Serves 4

SAUSAGE ARTICHOKE PIE

INGREDIENTS:

16 sheets phyllo dough, buttered

1 ½ cups butter, melted

18 medium artichoke bottoms, drained

8 medium Italian sausages, casing removed

3 lbs. ricotta cheese

6 large eggs, beaten

1 ½ cups grated parmesan cheese

1 ½ cups black olives, pitted

DIRECTIONS:

Brush the insides of a large spring form pan with butter. Then take four buttered phyllo sheets and place them in the middle of the pan going out over the rim. Repeat this so that all four quadrants are covered. Make sure the phyllo dough fits the bottom and sides of the spring form pan.

Add the drained artichoke bottoms, pat dry and lay them all over the bottom of the pan, concave side up.

In a medium frying pan, heat the olive oil and add the sausage (casings removed) breaking into small pieces and continue to cook until done. Add to pan on top of the artichoke bottoms.

Next, add the ricotta cheese to a medium mixing bowl, stir in the six beaten eggs and parmesan cheese, then fold in the whole, pitted black olives. Place mixture over sausage, smooth evenly to the sides.

SAUSAGE ARTICHOKE PIE
(CONTINUED)

Take any phyllo dough that is hanging over the edge of the pan and tuck it in between the pan and the phyllo dough. Brush the edge of the phyllo dough with butter.

Place in a 375^0 oven for fifty to sixty minutes, until edges and top are golden brown.

Serves 12

GRILLED CHICKEN COUSCOUS

INGREDIENTS:

4 chicken breast halves, boneless and skinless

1 large lemon, juiced

¼ cup olive oil, 1 inch thick

1 tsp. garlic, minced

1 tbs. fresh oregano, chopped

1 ½ cups couscous

2 cups chicken broth, bring to a boil

1 bunch green onions, cuisinart

3 tbs. fresh oregano, cuisinart

¼ cup lemon juice, whisk

2 tbs. honey, whisk

2 tsp. Dijon mustard, whisk

¾ cup olive oil, whisk

Godmother salt and some pepper, to taste

¼ cup almonds or cashews, toasted

DIRECTIONS:

In a medium-sized bowl, add couscous, pour in 2 cups boiling chicken broth, cover and set aside.

Marinate boneless, skinless chicken breasts in olive oil, lemon juice, garlic, and oregano for at least 1 hour. Grill over barbecue or on a hot pancake griddle, 3 to 4 minutes each side. Let cool.

GRILLED CHICKEN COUSCOUS
(CONTINUED)

In a food processor, medium chop green onions and fresh oregano.

Place on pancake griddle or small frying pan with olive oil, and grill to brown on both sides, Set aside, cool, and flake apart.

Fluff couscous with a fork. Toss with grilled, flaked green onion-oregano mx. Cut grilled chicken into thin slices.

Make dressing, whisking lemon juice, honey, salt, pepper, and olive oil together. Toss chicken slices and couscous together with dressing. Top with toasted almonds or cashews.

Serves 4

FUSILLI NESTA

INGREDIENTS:

1 lb. spinach fusilli

1 ½ cups cream

½ lb. fontina cheese, shredded

3 tbs. pesto sauce

1/8 tsp. white pepper

½ cup pignolia, (pine nuts) toasted

DIRECTIONS:

In a large pot, bring 6 quarts of salted water to a boil.

In a medium sauce pan, heat the cream. Stir in the shredded fontina cheese and 3 tablespoons of pesto sauce. Stir over medium heat until melted. Stir in white pepper. Cover and set aside.

Place 1 lb. of spinach fusilli in boiling water. Cook until al dente (8 to 10 minutes). (remember "tender but firm to the bite.")

Drain pasta, and place in a serving bowl. Pour over fontina cheese, toss well and garnish with toasted pignolis.

Serves 6

'HOUDINI' HAD NOTHING ON
THE GODMOTHER

Our first kitchen was a new, very shining, fully-equipped catering truck. The beauty of this set-up was our ability to back the van into the client's yard, patio, or driveway, and then cater a full service event without having to use the clients' kitchen…. Clients were beyond thrilled with the idea that they could present a 'neat home' to their guests, before and after the party. And if necessary, we could created an instant café by putting a few tables and chairs around the van, plug in the boom-box and it was instant party-time on wheels.

However, it was a test of fortitude and skill to move this huge truck around. I never really learned how to drive it, and certainly never did I manage to back it up. Fortunately, Duane or Marlys was always around to handle that challenge.

It's a remarkable thing that most hostesses, no matter what they economic status, religion, or cultural background, need to be 'perfect' when entertaining. They want their guests to think their house is always awaiting Vogue for a photo-shoot….no matter what time of day – kids, dogs, broken pipes, dirty dishes, garbage in not out, dirty laundry, piled up mail, none of these is to be addressed the night of a party. So all that stuff is hidden and the kitchen looks spotless. Our van kept this image alive for these dreamers. The guests could walk into the kitchen for a glass of water without the hostess slamming the door in their face for fear of seeing a dirty stove. No dirty pots or pans or dishes. Never a towel out of place. Walla!!! a great meal is served. Houdini and the Godmother, what a team!!!

The van had so many uses...I was a bit handicapped by my inability to drive it competently. However, I did manage to find an easy spot for parking, where I could pull in and out without difficulty. It was located at Pacific Coast Highway and Topanga Canyon on the property where Malibu Mercedes operated. (they have since changed their name to Malibu Motors and moved to Santa Monica) John, Albert, and their little brother Henry own and operate this very honorable car repair company. They ate well in exchange for allowing me to sell food every day for about two or three hours.

That's where I met Joe. At least four times a week, he'd stop by the van and take home dinner.

Chicken enchilada, moussaka, honey glazed carrots, chinese chicken strips with pea pods, broccoli with olive oil and garlic, parmesan scalloped potatoes. Quite a gourmet selection from a van!!!!!!!!

One day, Joe asked if I thought it was possible for the van to maneuver his driveway, a very winding, narrow and difficult one, even for the average car. He and his wife had discussed using the van for a party and his wife would be so thrilled because, (here it comes), "the kitchen would be clean" I checked out the driveway, and concluded it was more important to get the account than to acknowledge the fear of taking down half his house with the van.

We served 125 guests after a hold-your-breath drive to his front door for our first event. The kitchen remained spotless and the guests never realized the food was coming from a van outside, as they licked their plates cleaned. It was a smashing success. And unbelievably even with my lack of driving skills, his house remained intact.

Joe was a business agent for a very successful television star whose show, although I never watched it, was a big hit for years. His client, also renowned for her wonderful stage career in New York, came to all of their "van" parties. After about a year and a half of monthly "keep your kitchen clean parties", when I finally got the driveway down pat, I received a call from Joe's wife. They had to cancel the next party. The little bits of information I gathered left me sad. Allegedly there was a misappropriation of funds and Joe had been arrested. Within a few weeks, they sold their home, and we never heard another word from them.

As shocking as this news was, I am convinced that Joe would never have done anything to embarrass his family. He loved them very much. Articulate, intelligent, a loving husband and father with an enormous sense of humor and tons of style, he was a good man. I think about Joe, his wonderful wife and their two terrific kids a lot, and hope that they are once again together, healthy and happy.

MOUSSAKA

INGREDIENTS:

2 medium eggplant, sliced ¼ "thick

2 tbs. olive oil, for grilling

2 tbs. olive oil, for sauteeing

1 medium onion, diced

¾ lb. ground lamb

½ lb. Italian sausages, cooked and ground

½ cup red wine, for deglazing

2 tbs. tomato sauce

1/8 tsp. nutmeg

2 tsp. mint

Godmother salt and some pepper to taste

2 large eggs, beaten

½ cup grated parmesan cheese

¼ cup bread crumbs

TOPPING:

2 tbs. butter, melted

2 tbs. flour

1 ½ cups milk

2 large whole eggs, beaten

2 large egg yolks, beaten

1/8 tsp. nutmeg

3 tbs. grated parmesan cheese

MOUSSAKA
(CONTINUED)

DIRECTIONS:

Preheat oven to 375⁰.

In a hot cast iron skillet or pancake griddle, add olive oil and grill sliced eggplant on both sides until golden brown, pat dry of any excessive oil, and set aside.

Cook Italian sausage in a 375⁰ oven, uncovered, fifteen minutes each side, cool, and then blend in a food processor until well-ground.

In a large skillet, add the olive oil and sauté the chopped onion till soft, add the ground lamb, sauté till brown and then add the ground cooked sausage.

Add the red wine to the meat mixture, scraping the sides and the bottom till the pan is deglazed. Add the tomato sauce, parsley, mint, nutmeg and salt and pepper.

Remove pan from heat and stir in the parmesan cheese, bread crumbs, and the beaten eggs.

Spray an 8x8 baking dish with a vegetable spray. Line the bottom of the pan with half of the grilled eggplant. Pour the meat mixture over the eggplant, and pat into place till smooth. Place the other half of the grilled eggplant on top of the meat mixture.

In a small sauce pan, melt the butter and whisk in the flour, let bubble for 1 minute. Whisk in the milk, bring to a boil till thickened, removed from heat and slowly whisk in the beaten eggs and egg yolks. Stir in the parmesan cheese and nutmeg; pour over the grilled eggplant topping.

Bake uncovered 375⁰ for 30 to 40 minutes till golden brown.

CHICKEN ENCHILADAS

INGREDIENTS:

2 cups diced cooked chicken

2 cups sour cream

½ lb. cheddar cheese, shredded

½ lb. jack cheese, shreded

½ cup green onion, chopped

½ cup cilantro, chopped

¼ cup black olives, sliced

1 medium onion, diced

1 tsp. garlic, minced

12 oz. green chiles, chopped

12 oz. Italian tomatoes, chopped

½ cup chicken stock, salted to taste

1 tbs. cumin

½ tbs. oregano

¼ tbs. black pepper

9 6-inch tortillas, warmed

DIRECTIONS:

Enchiladas Sauce:

In a medium sauce pan, sauté the onions and garlic till just soft, add chopped green chilies, chopped Italian tomatoes, chicken stock, cumin, oregano, and black pepper. Bring sauce to a boil, lower to medium heat and cook for 20 minutes.

Preheat oven to 350°.

CHICKEN ENCHILADAS
(CONTINUED)

DIRECTIONS:

Spray a cast iron skillet with vegetable spray, and heat the corn tortillas 1 minute on each side, keep warm in a covered dish.

Spray an 8x8 baking dish with vegetable spray and line bottom of pan with 2 whole corn tortillas and 1 other tortilla cut in half to cover the rest of the pan's bottom. Ladle cooked enchilada sauce over tortillas, till they are well-covered (6 to 8 ounces).

Dot the sauced tortillas with 1 cup of sour cream, half of the diced chicken, half of each of the green onions, chopped cilantro, sliced black olives and ¼ cup mixed shredded cheddar and jack cheese.

Repeat the last layer starting with corn tortillas.

For the last layer, cover the top with the two whole and one halved tortillas, the rest of the sauce and ½ cup shredded jack and cheddar cheese.

Bake uncovered in a 350⁰ oven for thirty minutes, or until top cheese is melted and slightly golden.

Serves 6

CHINESE CHICKEN STRIPS
WITH PEA PODS

INGREDIENTS:

4 halved chicken breasts, boneless and skinless

1 tbs. Chinese five-spice seasoning

½ lb. snow peas

1/8 cup toasted sesame seeds

THE DRESSING:

1 orange, juice only

1 tsp. lemon juice

2 ounces rice wine vinegar

1 tsp. fresh ginger, grated

1 clove garlic, minced

1 tbs. orange marmalade

½ cup peanut oil

Godmother salt to taste

DIRECTIONS:

Preheat oven to 400⁰.

Place 4 halves of the boneless, skinless chicken breasts on a cookie sheet and rub Chinese five-spice over the top of each. Bake in 400⁰ oven for fifteen to twenty minutes, until just done.

Breasts will feel firm to the touch.

Let cool.

CHINESE CHICKEN STRIPS WITH PODS
(CONTINUED)

Remove stem ends and string on snow peas. Place peas in boiling water for 1 minute. Drain and immediately plunge in ice water for ten minutes, then drain.

In small skillet, place 1/8 cup of sesame seeds and cook over medium heat until they are golden brown. Set aside to cool.

Cut cooled chicken breasts across the grain, into ½-inch strips.

Toss chicken strips, pea pods and sesame seeds with Chinese dressing:

In a small saucepan, put lemon juice, orange juice, rice wine vinegar, grated ginger, garlic and orange marmalade. Cook over medium heat until marinade is slightly reduced (about ten minutes). Let cool.

Whisk ½ cup of peanut oil into reduced marinade. Pour over chicken strips.

HINT – After cooking and draining snow peas, beans, asparagus and broccoli, plunge them into ice water. This will stop the cooking process and holds the green color.

Serves 6

PARMESAN SCALLOPED POTATOES

INGREDIENTS:

4 large white or red rose potatoes, peeled

2 tbs. butter, melted

2 tbs. flour

2 cups low-fat milk

1 tsp. Godmother salt

½ tsp. pepper

½ cup parmesan cheese

DIRECTIONS:

In a medium saucepan, melt 2 tablespoons of butter and whisk in the flour. Stir constantly for two minutes; do not let brown. Pour in the low-fat milk, salt, and pepper and whisk until mixture is smooth.

Heat over medium heat, whisk frequently, till mixture is thick and silky. Remove from heat and whisk in parmesan cheese.

Preheat oven to 350°.

Wash, peel and slice potatoes. Spray an 8x8 baking dish with a vegetable spray and arrange 1/3 of the sliced potatoes, top with parmesan sauce. Continue the same with the next two layers.

Cover pan with foil and bake covered at 375° for thirty minutes. Uncover and bake at 375° for fifty to sixty minutes, till tender and golden brown.

Great served with lamb, chicken or turkey.

Serves 4

HONEY-GLAZED CARROTS

INGREDIENTS:

6 medium carrots, peeled and sliced

2 quarts salted water, bring to a boil

2 tsp. lemon juice

1 ½ tbs. honey

½ tsp. fresh dill, finely minced

DIRECTIONS:

Place peeled and sliced carrots into boiling water. Cook for 5 to 8 minutes until tender, drain.

In a medium-size bowl, place the lemon juice, honey and dill. Add the hot, drained carrots, toss until well-coated, then serve.

Serves 4

WHAT GOES AROUND
ABSOLUTELY COMES AROUND

Cosimo Sherman, one of our more discriminating foodies, and a Malibu kid was born in 1980, the same year the Godmother was launched.

When he was two years old he walked into the shop holding his dad Eric's hand and became an instant "regular." He claims he can remember very clearly many things about those years: that the shop was "very bright and colorful," he loved the "white salad" and the "funny bread," and was always happy to be there.

The "white salad" is celeriac salad. The "funny bread" is our own zucchini pie. This kid had a nose for good food before he knew how to talk. He never ate a McDonald's hamburger, but more importantly, never wanted one either. Although he wasn't crazy about zucchini, he had no problem with "funny bread".

His parents, Eric and Genie Sherman chose the Godmother Café as the ideal spot to tell Cos that they were expecting another child. As he chewed his "funny bread," they broke the news. Cos immediately demanded a baby sister. Genie assured him that it was out of her hands. Rocky was born in 1982, and Cos was content to keep him as long as Rocky ate "funny bread".

Rocky picked up the message in utero, because as soon as he could crawl he started eating his own little selections of Godmother favorites. These kids were my "celebrities". They were the youngest to ever eat Godmother food as part of their regular diet until my Kailani Kea (age two) took the title from them this year.

A Saturday afternoon wouldn't have been complete without the Shermans at their regular table.

They became part of the ambiance of the café, eating and laughing for hours, enjoying each other's company. Soon Cos started to expand his tastes. When he turned eight, he added the grilled vegetable sandwich with pesto to his favorite list. Each year, another Godmother specialty was added. For his eighteenth birthday, the Shermans, surprised him with a bash at the café and we enjoyed all of his mouth-watering childhood foods.

He and Rocky returned the favor for their parents twentieth wedding anniversary. We catered a spectacular surprise party at their home with ice sculptures, Dixieland bands and of course 'white salad', 'funny bread' and the pesto sandwiches.

In 2004 Rocky had his twenty-second birthday party at the café with the whole Sherman clan laughing and bringing warmth and love to us once again.

EGGPLANT PARMESAN
(one of my personal favorites)

INGREDIENTS:

1 large eggplant

1 cup of flour

1 ½ tbs. Godmother salt

2 large eggs

¼ cup whole milk

¾ cup of virgin oil

½ cup of Godmother marinara sauce

1 ½ cup grated parmesan cheese

2 cups of shredded mozzarella cheese

DIRECTIONS:

Cut off both ends of eggplant

Slice eggplant into ¼ inch thick rounds.

Dredge in flour and salt mixture and set aside

Heat griddle or frying pan on medium to high heat

In a medium-size mixing bowl, beat eggs and milk together

Heat a thin layer of oil in frying pan or on a grill.

Dip the eggplant into the mixture and add to grill or frying pan.. Making sure that each piece does not overlap...brown and cook 5 to 7 minutes each side

Drain on paper towels

Repeat until all eggplant is cooked

EGGPLANT PARMESAN
(CONTINUED)

In a 9x13 pan add olive oil and line bottom of pan with cooked eggplant slices. Spread ¾ marinara sauce on top of eggplant, top with 1 cup of shredded mozzarella cheese and ½ cup parmesan cheese.

Repeat layers

At approximately an inch from the top of the pan, add the final layer... grilled eggplant, remaining marinara sauce and ½ grated parmesan cheese only.

Bake in 375° degree oven, uncovered thirty to forty minutes till top is slightly brown and bubbly

Serves 6

CELERY ROOT SALAD

INGREDIENTS:

1 lb. celery root or celeriac

1 ½ tsp. Godmother salt

1 ½ tsp. lemon juice

paper towels

DRESSING INGREDIENTS:

¾ cup sour cream

¼ cup of mayonnaise

2 tbs. dijon mustard

1/8 cup Chardonnay wine

1 tsp. celery seed

DIRECTIONS:

Peel celery root, cut into quarters into a food processor with a fine shredding disc.

When all celery root is finely shredded, toss with salt and lemon juice till well coated. Cover and let sit for a half hour.

In a large mixing bowl add sour cream, mayonnaise, mustard, wine and celery seed, whisk all ingredients together unti well blended. Place celery root into a strainer, drain well, place on paper towel to dry, then place in bowl with dressing, toss till well covered.

Chill for at least two hours. (for very tender celery root, chill longer.)

6 servings

PAVAROTTI & ME

This is one of those rare times that I actually did cook!!

"Basta con queste cose. Tu sei molto meglio di me. Il cibo e'magnifico." ("Enough of this, you are much better than me. This food is magnificent.") These words, said in both Italian and English, came from the lips of Luciano Pavarotti, probably the greatest tenor in the world.

He and I were standing in Carolyn and Joe Sargent's kitchen, preparing linguini with garlic and tomatoes for the kids and staff of the Free Arts Clinic, the non-profit organization, founded by Carolyn, which helps abused kids.

Every couple of months, Joe and Carolyn invited these kids to their beach house in Malibu for special luncheons ... and this one was sure special, with Pavorotti in attendance.

Pavarotti was a house guest at the Sargent's home because he had just wrapped the movie, *Yes. Yes. Georgio* directed by Joe.

We were actually cooking together. As I chopped and sautéed, he tasted and sang. I kept pinching myself to make sure I wasn't dreaming.

While I was cooking the linguini and sautéing the olive oil and garlic, Pavarotti was chopping the Roma tomatoes, when he suddenly dropped his knife, looked at me and said, "You make it seem so easy." My heart was in atrial fibrillation (beating rapidly). I was afraid he was going to hear the noise.

I love opera. Although I'm a Callas fanatic, and thus have trouble fully appreciating other opera greats. Luciano Pavarotti isn't chopped liver, and I thoroughly respect his enormous vocal talent, his magnificent stage presence and his colorful career.

When we said goodbye, he slipped one of his albums under my arm. He had inscribed it personally to me. In Italian he wrote "Lei e'meglio di me" ("You are so much better than I"). I've framed it, of course, to remind myself why I do what I do, and how much fun I have doing it.

Luciano Pavarotti died on September 6, 2007. The beauty and brilliance of his voice will stay in my heart forever. I will always remember the day we made pasta together.

HERB SPINACH RICOTTA
STUFFED CHICKEN BREASTS

INGREDIENTS:

4 half chicken breasts, boneless with skin, pat dry

2 tbs. butter

1 cup ricotta cheese

½ cup parmesan cheese

8 oz. chopped frozen spinach, defrosted

¼ cup fresh basil, chopped

1 tbs. fresh oregano, minced

1 tbs. fresh mint, chopped

¼ cup pine nuts, toasted

DIRECTIONS:

In a medium bowl, add the ricotta cheese, parmesan cheese, chopped fresh herbs and toasted pine nuts. Take the defrosted spinach and squeeze all excess water out and add to cheese herb mixture. Mix all ingredients together until well blended.

Preheat oven to 375^0

Take boneless chicken breast and loosen the skin on one side to make a pouch between the breast and the skin.

Divide spinach-herb-ricotta mixture into four even portions. Take each measured spinach-herb-cheese mixture and stuff it into each pouch under the chicken skin. Smooth skin over the herb mixture, and with your hands, cup each chicken breast until it is a smooth oblong stuffed breast.

HERB SPINACH RICOTTA
STUFFED CHICKEN BREASTS
(CONTINUED)

Place breasts in a baking dish, brushing each breast with melted butter.

Place in a 375^0 oven for 30 minutes, or until skin is golden brown.

Serve with a brown or wild rice dish.

Serves 4

LINGUINI WITH BAKED ROMA TOMATOES

INGREDIENTS:

1 lb. linguine

¼ cup olive oil

½ cup olive oil

1 tbs. garlic, chopped

12 medium roma tomatoes, quartered lengthwise

2 tbs. fresh oregano or rosemary, finely chopped

2 tsp. Godmother salt

6 grinds fresh black pepper, coarsely ground

DIRECTIONS:

Preheat oven to 400°.

Add 1 pound of linguine to boiling, salted water, cook 8 to 10 minutes, till pasta is al dente (tender but firm to the bite). Drain and rinse with cold water. Toss pasta with ¼ cup olive oil and set aside.

In a large baking pan, add the quartered-lengthwise Roma tomatoes, olive oil, freshly chopped oregano or rosemary, garlic, salt and ground black pepper. Toss the tomatoes till well coated and then place in a 400° oven for 20 to 30 minutes. Tomatoes should be browned slightly and juicy.

When tomatoes are done, toss in the linguine and place back in oven for 8 to 10 minutes, till pasta is hot. Serve with freshly grated parmesan cheese.

Serves 6

STUFFED BREAST OF TURKEY

INGREDIENTS:

3 lbs. breast of turkey breast, with a pocket

4 cups Italian bread, 1 inch cubes

1 cup cream

4 medium Italian sausage, cooked, ground

1 medium onion, chopped

1 cup Parmesan cheese

1 cup spinach, cooked and chopped

1 cup peas, frozen, defrosted

2 large eggs, beaten

½ cup fresh basil, chopped

½ tsp. sage

1 cup pinenuts, toasted

3 medium eggs, hard boiled

2 oz. brandy

1 tbs. kitchen bouquet

1 tbs. Dijon mustard

2 tsp. rosemary, finely chopped

1 tbs. capers

DIRECTIONS:

Preheat oven to 450°.

Have butcher make a pouch in breast of turkey breast

Soak Italian bread in cup of cream for a few minutes.

STUFFED BREAST OF TURKEY
(CONTINUED)

To make a stuffing, mix together cream soaked bread, beaten eggs, ground cooked sausage, parmesan cheese, onions, cooked chopped spinach, peas, pine nuts, basil and sage. Place half of sausage stuffing inside breast, then place 3 peeled hard boiled eggs in a row down the center. Place remaining sausage stuffing on top of hard boiled eggs.

With metal or wooden skewers, close the open end of the breast by threading the skewer in and out of the open edges. Pat dry and place in a medium baking dish. Make a paste by blending the brandy, kitchen bouquet, Dijon mustard, minced rosemary and capers. Brush the top of the turkey roast with the mixture.

Place in a 450^0 oven uncovered for 20 minutes, reduce heat to 350^0 and 1 cup chicken broth and ½ cup white wine, cover with foil, bake until tender (2 – 2 ½ hr).

Serves 6

BROCCOLI WITH OLIVE OIL
& GARLIC

INGREDIENTS:

1 lb. broccoli, cut into flowerettes

2 quarts salted water, boiling

¼ cup olive oil heated

2 cloves of garlic minced

DIRECTIONS:

Place sliced broccoli flowerettes into salted boiling water. Cook for 5 to 8 minutes, till desired tenderness, and drain.

In a large skillet, heat the olive oil and sauté the minced garlic until just soft. Add the drained broccoli and toss in the skillet until well-coated.

Place in a serving bowl with parmesan cheese on the side.

Serves 4

AH, MALIBU!

It's hard to know in Malibu
Where to go and what to do;
From lofty peaks to golden strand,
Myriad attractions on every hand.
Great sharks that have no enemies;
Tide pools with flowering anemones

Everywhere artists with an easel
A friendly bookstore known as Diesel;
The Godmother creating new dishes
All three-star and nutritious;
Far out at sea looms Catalina,
Yachts racing home to the marina.

Brown pelicans flying in echelon,
Alert for sardines to pounce upon;
Gray whales, almost always in a pair,
Spouting misty plumes high in the air,
And surfers, we count them by the score,
Riding massive waves towards the shore.

Why waste a fortune on a cruise or tour?
Malibu memories will long endure;
Come down at dawn for the pearly light,
Stay for the brilliant skies at night.
Forget Rio, Hawaii or Kuala Lumpur,
Malibu has all they have, and more!

BY MALIBU'S OWN BELOVED POET
EXTRAORDINAIRE,
ROY RINGER

ONE OF A KIND

Robert Altman, Academy Award-winning director/producer was the best in his field. He was called prolific, curmudgeonly, irreplaceable, a renegade, a genius, certainly a legend ... He was indeed a true original. He gave us some of the most incredibly crafted and brilliant independent films throughout the years; *Mash, Nashville, The Player, Short-Cuts, Cookie's Fortune, Gosford Park,* to name but a few. His last film, *Prairie Home Companion* with a great cast of characters offered us so many moments of delicious amusement.

His death at the end of 2006 left a huge hole in the universe.

Independent film production is tough. You have to find your own money to finance the films, but if you can accomplish that little task you don't have to put up with the massive egos of those who head studios and their "assistants", all of whom have a very common bottom line ... making money. Quality isn't even on the agenda.

Bob Altman was only about quality.

He gave me another life lesson. He never did any film he didn't want to do ... and was my inspiration for 'hanging in there'.

This talented man had a stable of actors who would drop everything if he called. His reputation for quality and professionalism is universal. His ability to understand and appreciate actors was cherished.

Actors became actors to act. It's not about making mega bucks because most actors never make mega bucks ... the percentage of working actors who earn a livable wage is very very small, the percentage of working actors who make mega-bucks is even smaller. That doesn't mean that those who make mega-salaries are not talented.

229

Many are; they are just luckier and sometimes in the right place at the right time.

Finding someone who understands actors as well as Bob Altman did, is like finding water in the Gobi desert.

I go to the movies to lose myself for a couple of hours. Movies are better than any therapy I could ever get ... relieves my stress, relaxes my tension, and makes me a much happier soul when I see a good film. There isn't a Bob Altman film that didn't make me lose myself for the moment.

He was a very unique person, and so is his beautiful wife, who was at his side for almost fifty years. It was so apparent to anyone who spent two seconds with them, that they not only loved each other but really liked being together. Kathryn has a wonderful wit. She's quick and clever and so very knowledgeable about the world and life in particular. She is one of my heros. I consider them friends, and have enjoyed the many years that we have catered for them and their wonderful family.

Despite "A" list names at their events, there was never any egos out of control at their home. It was always comfortable whether the room was filled with celebrities, friends, or just family and neighborhood friends.

And then ONE NIGHT...

Valerie was preparing the buffet, and at the other end of the room, the guests were listening to a hugely popular country-western star who was playing guitar and singing some of the songs he has written.

Sitting close to the kitchen where Valerie and the staff were preparing dinner, was an "icon" of the music industry ... someone that Valerie didn't know or recognize because he was famous before she was born and although she has an affinity for the '40s and '50s, she has no interest in his specialty… "big bands."

This "icon" has appeared all over the world, selling millions and millions of albums. He was the most popular band leader of his day; however, he was also famous for his proclivity of marrying the most glamorous stars of that era.

The country-western singer was midway into his song when the "icon" suddenly turns to Valerie and says in a very loud voice, "Who the hell is that?"

Valerie, although a bit stunned by his remark, immediately whispered the singer's name into his ear, hoping to reduce the volume of his reply.

"He stinks," came the reply, just as loud as the first comment.

Valerie felt blessed that night, because the guests appeared so enraptured with the music that they didn't hear the dialogue going on at the end of the room. Maybe they did, but because they knew the "icon's" reputation for being very cantankerous and annoying, no one reacted.

The staff moved quickly to get the food served so that the music would stop for dinner and hopefully the "icon" would shut up.

It worked!

We learned later that the "icon's" behavior that evening was so very typical. Always a difficult personality, he was tolerated because of his talent. Now we know the reason for the many wives.

Somewhere between the appetizers of ahi tempura and the sit-down dinner of baby lamb chops with orzo and buttered sage, we saw the "icon" enjoying the food and not another disgruntled word came out of this octogenarian's mouth.

If people are miserable when they are young, they don't change as they age ... they just get worse.

AHI TEMPURA

INGREDIENTS:

8 oz. ahi steak, 1 ½ inches thick

1 package nori sheets

1 package tempura mix

1 package panko flakes (bread crumbs)

1 quart canola oil

THE DIP:

2/3 cup mayonnaise

2 tsp. wasabi paste

½ lemon, juice only

DIRECTIONS:

Cut the ahi into four long pieces. Wrap each piece in a sheet of nori, leaving 1 inch of nori at each end, and twist it closed.

Place the ahi back in the refrigerator to chill.

Make three cups of *tempura batter according to directions, using ice water only.

Sprinkle panko evenly over bottom of a sheet pan.

In an 8 inch sauce pan, heat canola oil to 375°.

Remove nori-wrapped ahi from refrigerator, and dip in tempura batter, holding both ends.

Dip until well-covered, and then roll in panko crumbs.

Place one piece at a time in hot oil and fry until deep golden brown.

AHI TEMPURA
(CONTINUED)

Remove and drain on paper towels.

Cut each roll in half at an angle, serve with wasabi mayo.

WASABI MAYO:

In small bowl, whip together mayonnaise, lemon juice and wasabi paste.

Place in a small dish next to each ahi roll and serve immediately.

Serves 4

* Use a good commercial brand tempura mix or here is a recipe I like very much...

TEMPURA BATTER:

1 large egg, yolk only

1 ½ cups very very cold water

1 cup of flour

Mix the yolk and water. Add flour all at once and mix slightly. Don't over mix ... you'll know if you've done it correctly if there are large lumps of flour and a rim of dust around the bowl.

Mix the batter in small amounts only.

MARSAMI'S RICOTTA PIE

INGREDIENTS FOR CRUST:

2 cups flour

1 stick butter (1/4 lb.)

3 eggs (2 yolks, 1 whole)

¼ cup milk

1 tsp. vanilla extract

¼ cup sugar

THE FILLING:

3 lbs. ricotta cheese

1 ½ cups sugar

10 eggs, separated

2 tbs. lemon extract

2 tbs. lemon juice with grated rind

2 tbs. orange juice with grated rind

1 cup candied citron

THE CRUST:

Cut butter into flour. Add beaten eggs, milk, vanilla, sugar.

Knead and roll out onto slightly floured board.

Mix all ingredients and place into 10" cake pan, about 2" deep. Criss-cross strips with remaining pie crust.

Heat in 350⁰ oven for 60 minutes.

Enjoy with strong cappuccino or espresso.

Serve 8

Molto bene!!!

ROSEMARY GRILLED CHICKEN

INGREDIENTS:

4 half chicken breasts, skin on

4 sprigs of fresh rosemary

¼ cup olive oil

1 medium lemon, juiced

1 tsp. garlic

DIRECTIONS:

Place the chicken breasts in a baking dish.

In a small bowl, place the lemon juice, crumbled sprigs of fresh rosemary, and garlic and whisk in the olive oil. Pour over the chicken breasts and marinate in the refrigerator for 4 hours or overnight.

Grill chicken breasts on a pre-heated hot cast iron skillet or a pancake griddle. Cook 3 to 4 minutes on each side, until center is cooked.

Serve on a bed of red pepper sauce.

Serves 4

GRILLED BABY LAMB CHOPS

INGREDIENTS:

12 small, thick baby lamb chops

1 tsp. minced garlic

1 ½ tsp. chopped fresh mint

2 tsp. sugar

¼ cup boiling water

2/3 cup apple cider vinegar

1 tsp. coarse-ground black pepper

2/3 cup virgin olive oil

DIRECTIONS:

In a medium bowl, add garlic, chopped mint, and sugar. Pour ¼ cup boiling water over ingredients, and steep for twenty minutes.

Stir in apple cider, vinegar, black pepper and olive oil.

Place lamb chops in a baking pan, top with marinade, cover and refrigerate at least four hours or overnight.

Grill marinated baby lamb chops over a medium heat three to five minutes per side.

Meat thermometer should read 140^0 to 150^0.

4 servings

ROASTED RED PEPPER SAUCE

INGREDIENTS:

1 red bell pepper

1 tbs. balsamic vinegar

1 tsp. brown sugar

¼ cup of virgin olive oil

Godmother salt and some pepper to taste

DIRECTIONS:

Roast the red pepper over a high gas flame. Sear pepper until skin is black on all sides. Take off heat and place in a small paper bag and seal tight. It should steam in the bag for 30 minutes. Remove pepper and peel off chard skin, remove inner seed. Rough chop and place in a food processor along with balsamic vinegar, brown sugar, salt and pepper.

Remove mixture from processor, place in a bowl and whisk in the olive oil.

Serve chilled or at room temperature.

4 servings

ORZO WITH BROWN BUTTER SAGE

INGREDIENTS:

2 cups orzo

1 tsp. salt

¼ cup virgin olive oil

2/3 cup sweet butter

1 cup sage leaves, chopped

Fresh ground black pepper to taste

DIRECTIONS:

Add salt to four quarts of water and bring to a boil. Add two cups orzo and bring back to a boil. Cook 8 to 10 minutes, until firm. Drain, rinse with hot water and drain till almost dry.

In a medium sauce pan, add the olive oil and butter. Bring to almost a boil, then remove from heat. Stir in chopped sage and let cook one to two minutes. Pour over orzo. Toss until well coated. Add fresh ground pepper to taste.

Serve with a sprig of fresh sage on the side.

Serves 4

AUNT EMMA'S CHEESECAKE

INGREDIENTS:

6 eggs, separated

1 cup sugar

1 pint sour cream

2 large packages Philadelphia Cream Cheese

½ lemon juice only

½ tsp. vanilla

DIRECTIONS:

Beat egg white and set aside.

Mix all ingredients in a large bowl until smooth, then fold in egg whites.

On bottom of pan, mix:

¾ cup graham cracker crumbs

2 tbs. butter

2 tbs. sugar

Mix well and lay on bottom of ungreased pan. Pour in mixture. Leave cake to settle before baking for 1 hour.

Bake at 325⁰ for 1 hour.

"OPEN A NEW WINDOW, OPEN A NEW DOOR"

When the show, *Mame*, starring Angela Lansbury opened on Broadway at the Winter Garden Theater on May 24, 1966, I went nuts.

Opening night tickets were impossible to find but I managed to be in the orchestra section, front row center on May 25th, the very next night. That was the beginning of a long odyssey for me.

What a show! Touching, teary, heart-wrenching story, beautifully performed by all, with show stopping music spreading joy throughout the audience. *Mame* was an incredible delightful musical that took New York and me by storm.

Watching Angela Lansbury and Bea Arthur perform the fabulous *Bosum Buddies* routine from Act two, was to watch musical theater at its very best.

I saw the show twenty-seven times in the three years it was on Broadway. I went with family, friends, and even with total strangers if I had too. A trifle obsessive? No, it was just terrific musical theater. So seldom do you watch such overall perfection.

It made me happy; lifted me when I was tired and frustrated, put a whole new prospective on the world, New York and whatever was happening in my life at that moment.

I kept "opening new windows" and finding "new hope". When I got my hands on one of the show's important props, the bugle, I had all of the dates I had seen the show engraved on the front of it.

The bugle now resides at the Gershwin Theater in New York. But I'm getting ahead of my story.

I was fortunate to meet Angela Lansbury and her charming husband Peter during the run of the show. She saw me so often from the stage that she probably thought I worked there.

Fast forward to California, twenty years later, and The Godmother.

Our kids were singing "We need a little Christmas" and "Open a New Window" both from *Mame* while other kids were singing nursery rhymes.

Because of Mame, a family tradition began.

I bought sterling silver goblets at Tiffany's (tiny ones for the kids) and on birthdays everyone had a splash of champagne before school or work…. Such a Mame thing to do. "Live, live, life is a banquet and most poor sob's are starving to death."*

One morning, at The Godmother Café, a darling looking, dapper gentlemen, comfortably dressed in casual khaki slacks and a hunter green T- shirt, brown shining loafers sporting new pennies and no socks, inquired about our catering services.

We liked each other instantly and talked for a long time about Malibu, food, wine and Broadway. Suddenly I realized that I was sitting across the table from one of the men (the other being Robert E. Lee) who wrote the play Auntie Mame and ultimately the book for "Mame" the show.

Jerome Lawrence was sitting in my Café talking to me about doing a party at his home. Doesn't get any better than this, I thought.

Do I tell him now that I've seen the play twenty-seven times? Of course not! He'd probably leave immediately thinking I was a bit tilted and emotionally incapable of handling a party for 100.

I could barely control myself. I was like a kid who was told that I could eat all the cream puffs and ice cream I wanted and never gain another pound. Such ecstacy!!!

Would Jerry Herman who wrote the music be there? Would Angela Lansbury? Bea Arthur?

That funny Jane Connell who played the poor Agnes Gooch or Frankie Michaels that dear boy who played the young nephew Patrick. My head was spinning.

And so they were, and so was the original winding staircase from the show...built right into his home....

As guests started to arrive, walking down that beautifully mahogany staircase, that Angela used for those many wonderful *Mame* years in New York, Jerry's assistant sat at the piano and played "It's Today," which is the opening number that Angela sang as she descended the stairs.

I felt as though I was dreaming. It was so unreal....20 years later I'm sitting in the midst of the world of Mame.

What wonderful good fortune I have had knowing amazing people like the very talented Jerry Lawrence, who also wrote *Inherit the Wind* and *Dear World* and became a dear, dear friend.

After a series of unfortunate illnesses, he was confined to his home for several years and it became a weekly ritual for some of us, his closest friends, to join him every Wednesday night for dinner.

His reminiscences of his years in show business were filled with colorful stories. Those were the days before constant "paparazzi"; the indiscretions and the "mistakes" were much more tolerated and respected. You got away with so much because there was an unwritten respect for privacy ...would you believe?

Jerry told us some very delicious stories about some of the most intriguing celebrities of the day.

Before we sat down for dinner, however, on Wednesday nights we had to take the "oath", never to repeat what he said around that table, "What you hear here, stays here".

When his house burned in 1993 during one of Malibu's most destructive firestorms, he lost all of his memorabilia; posters, photos of the many many women who were playing Mame currently around the world; scrap books,, recordings and scripts...fortunately because of loving and devoted friends and co-workers, actors and officianatos of the Broadway theater around the world, he managed to re-collect many of his precious memories before he died.

At his 80th birthday party, he was presented with the original Mame poster which was 15 feet high and had hung on the side of the Winter Garden Theater from the day the show opened. It came by truck convoy from New York.

My gift to him was the bugle. He was so touched by the gesture that he placed it on his beautifully crafted cedar table by his front door. It remained there until the day he died, when it was sent to the Gershwin Theater in New York as part of a Jerome Lawrence/Robert E. Lee exhibition and is on display in the lobby of the theater today.

The following plaque is attached to the display:

"This is a bugle from the original Broadway production of *Mame*, book by Jerome Lawrence and Robert E. Lee based on their stage play, *Auntie Mame*. There is a marked dent and an absence of a mouth piece due to an accident during one performance. At the top of the staircase one evening, the bugle slipped from Miss Lansbury's hands bounced on the stage and the mouthpiece went flying into the orchestra pit. The bugle received the visible dent from the fall and Miss Lansbury took it with her that evening as a memento. However, waiting at the stage door was a young girl (that's me) who'd seen the show over ten times. Lansbury recognized the girl from the theater and promptly gave her the bugle as a thank you gesture for enjoying the show so often.

Over the next two years the girl would go on to see the show many more times (27 total). She would have the date engraved onto the bugle of each performance she attended.

Years later, this young girl would become the successful caterer in Malibu, California know as *The Godmother*. Dolores Rivellino became a longtime friend and catered many parties at the Lawrence Malibu home.

A tragic fire in 1993, in Malibu destroyed over 365 structures including Mr. Lawrence's home. Upon the completion of his rebuilding effort, "*The Godmother*" came to his birthday party with bugle in tow. She wanted him to have a replacement for the one he lost in the fire. And while the bugle has served well in the new Malibu home, Mr. Lawrence's family thought it would not only serve better at the Gershwin, but also Miss Rivellino a true fan of the show will be remembered."

Pretty cool!!!!

As much as he loved the theater, Jerry also loved good food and used any excuse to entertain in his lovely Malibu home overlooking the blue Pacific.

His all time favorites were our lamb stew, cannollonl, peasant sauce and sautéed scallops.

His generousity towards his friends and family was always evident in his extraordinary ability to make so many people happy, whether it was on the stage, or in his home. Somehow through the inexplicable way of life I ended up one of his closest friends. I'll miss him.

* From the book of *Auntie Mame* by Robert E. Lee and Jerome Lawrence

LAMB STEW

INGREDIENTS:

2 lbs. lamb shoulder, cut into 1 ½ cubes

½ cup of flour

¼ cup of extra virgin olive oil

2 shallots, minced

2 leeks, cleaned, sliced into ½ half rings

1 lb. pearl onions, peeled

4 stalks celery, diced

2 carrots peeled & diced

6 medium potatoes peeled, cut into quarters

1 cup dry red wine

3 cups vegetable broth

1 tsp. thyme

Godmother salt & some pepper to taste

DIRECTIONS:

Dredge lamb cubes into flour, sprinkle with salt & pepper.

Into six quart soup pot, add olive oil. Heat oil, and when very hot add floured lamb. Let brown till deep golden on all four sides. Add minced shallots, leeks, celery and cook till transluscent....five to eight minutes.

Pour in wine, stirring frequently to deglaze the pan, about 3 minutes. Add vegetable broth, add carrots, onions and potatoes and thyme. Cook on medium heat till stew comes to a boil.

Lower heat to simmer and continue to cook for 1 hour and 20 minutes.

Serves 4

JERRY'S SCALLOPS

INGREDIENTS:

1 lb. bay scallops

¾ cup of dry vermouth

2 cloves of garlic, minced

Godmother salt to taste

pepper to taste

2 tbs. minced Italian parsley

1 stick of sweet butter

DIRECTIONS:

In a medium size sauce pan, melt the butter. Add scallops and garlic. Sauté until golden brown-about one to 1 ½ minutes each side. Add vermouth and cook for additional 2 minutes. With a slotted spoon place scallops on platter. Turn heat on high and reduce juice by half, pour over scallops and add chopped parsley and salt and pepper.

Serve immediately

Serves 4

SPINACH CANNELLONI

INGREDIENTS:

24 6" crepes

1 ½ lbs. frozen chopped spinach, thawed and drained

2 lbs. ricotta cheese

3 large eggs, beaten

1 cup reggiano parmesan cheese

½ cup fontina cheese grated

¼ tsp. nutmeg, grated

BECHAMEL SAUCE:

½ cup butter, melted

½ cup flour, stir in butter

2 cups cream, stirred in

2 cups milk, stirred in

½ cup sherry, added

½ cup parmesan cheese added

1 cup sauce, marinara drizzled on top.

DIRECTIONS:

In a medium mixing bowl, add the ricotta cheese, eggs, parmesan cheese and nutmeg, stirring till well-blended. Squeeze spinach till all remaining moisture is gone, break apart and stir in to cheese mixture.

SPINACH CANNELLONI
(CONTINUED)

Lay the crepes out and on one edge, place two tablespoons spinach ricotta- mixture across the bottom, roll up and place seam side down in a 8x8 baking pan. Repeat until all the crepes are done

In a medium sauce pan, melt the butter and stir in flour...blend well. Continue to stir until bubbles form, three minutes.

Add cream, milk, and sherry and continue to cook till mixture is smooth and creamy. Remove from heat and stir in parmesan cheese.

Pour bechamel mixture over crepes, covering them half way...then spoon the peasant sauce in a line down the center of the crepe about 1" wide.

Place in 375⁰ oven uncovered 30 to 40 minutes till slightly browned.

Serves 12 or 24

PEASANT SAUCE

INGREDIENTS:

¼ cup of virgin olive oil

2 tbs. garlic, minced

20 medium Roma tomatos, peeled, seeded & chopped

12 oz. marinara sauce

¼ lb. prosciutto, julienned

2 tbs. oregano, dried

¼ cup parsley, finely chopped

pinch of Godmother salt

DIRECTIONS:

In a 4 quart sauce pan, add the olive oil and the minced garlic. Sauté 2 to 4 minutes, till slightly golden in color.

Add the peeled, seeded and chopped roma tomatoes and the marinara sauce.

(The best way to peel roma tomatoes is to place them in boiling water for 3 minutes, drain and plunge into cold water.)

Add the julienned prosciutto, oregano, salt and pepper. Simmer 45 minutes. Stir in chopped parsley just before adding linguini. Top with freshly grated reggiano parmesan cheese.

4 Servings.

THE GREEK SALAD

INGREDIENTS:

4 stalks celery cut into ½ pieces

½ red onion, finely sliced

1 medium green bell pepper, chop into 1 inch pieces

2 medium red bell peppers, chop into 1 inch pieces

2 medium cucumbers, peeled and seeded, cut into ½ length and the slice into ¼ slices

3 medium Roma tomatoes, quartered

1 cup Kalamaata olives

12 oz. feta cheese, cut into 1 inch pieces

2 tbs. lemon juice

pinch of Godmother salt

pinch of pepper

½ tsp. fresh oregano, finely chopped

½ cup of extra virgin olive oil

DIRECTIONS:

Place cut vegetables and olives in a medium size bowl.

In another small bowl, add lemon juice, oregano, salt and pepper and start slowly whisking in the olive oil. When well blended pour into bowl with vegetables and olives and toss until the vegetables are well covered.

Add the feta cheese

(Always serve cold salads with chilled forks)

Serves 6

THE GODMOTHER'S SPINACH SALAD

DRESSING:

1 ½ cups rice wine vinegar

3 cups peanut or canola oil

2 tbs. white onions, finely chopped

½ brown sugar, packed

2 tsp. dry mustard

Place onion, vinegar, brown sugar and dry mustard into a blender and run at medium speed. Drizzle in oil.

Makes 16 servings. Refrigerate and use as needed

INGREDIENTS:

12 cups of baby spinach leaves

½ red onion finely sliced

¾ cup crumbled soft gorgonzola cheese

½ cup spicy pecans*

Put baby spinach, onion, gorgonzola and stir gently with ½ cup of dressing. Add spicy pecans.

6 servings

* We make our own spicy pecans. It's not an easy recipe to explain. I would suggest you either buy them at a specialty store like William Sonoma or call us.

GODMOTHER'S SPECIAL MARINARA SAUCE....

INGREDIENTS:

¼ cup of virgin olive oil

Hand full of garlic minced

35 oz. can of imported Italian tomatoes

2-3 basil leaves, chopped

½ tsp. of oregano

Gomother salt and some black pepper to taste

DIRECTIONS:

In a large sauce pan, sauté garlic and olive oil. Add tomatoes, add water as needed. Add basil, oregano, salt & pepper. Bring to a boil. Then lower heat and let simmer for 30 minutes.

Serve on anything you desire

THE 'TOMATO BISQUE' SOUP

HERE IT IS!

Somewhere many pages back, I mentioned that this recipe appeared to Marlys in a dream. I honestly believe because of that, it would be impossible to duplicate outside the Godmother walls. Many have tried and actually a few have succeeded. We make no quarantees, however. You could hit it the first time. I have no scientific reason to explain it either, except its out of my hands and in the hands of some guardian Angels, I suspect.

Just about everyone in Malibu and places beyond, has tasted the Tomato Bisque. Sales of this soup managed to keep us afloat during most of Malibu's dramatic disasters; floods, massive slides, road closures and fires when so many took bodily risks to reach the shop for bowls of this delicious soup.

I swear on all that's good and holy, that every ingredient needed to prepare this soup is listed in the recipe and that the directions are precise and exactly the same ones used to prepare this soup at the café. Remember THIS is the recipe that made me a believer. It came to us through a dream and always tastes the same. I stopped trying to figure out the why's and how's, long ago.

TOMATO BISQUE SOUP

INGREDIENTS:

¼ cup butter

¼ cup cream

1 cup flour

1 cup chicken broth, salted to taste

28 oz. can of Italian tomatoes

1 small onion, diced

1 lb. honey

1 tsp. dill

1 tsp. marjoram

1 tsp. basil

1 tsp. oregano

2 tsp. parsley, chopped

DIRECTIONS:

In a two quart sauce-pan, melt the butter and then stir in the flour; stir frequently over medium heat for 3 minutes, do not brown.

Whisk in the cream and the chicken broth and stir until creamy.

Crush Italian tomatoes in a blender and pour into the cream mixture.

Add the remaining ingredients and herbs.

Simmer on low heat for 40 minutes, do not boil or soup will break.

Good luck!

Serves 8

AND THE SOUP PLAYS ON.........

Mike Fleetwood, from the famed Fleetwood Mac band, owes me $5.50 plus tax for a bowl of the Tomato Bisque soup.(1980's prices). There was a brief time when he was hanging around The Godmother Shop almost on a daily basis because his then-wife, Sara, a real sweetheart, worked next door at TOPS, a unique gift store. Tomato Bisque was their favorite. We kept a running tab for them, and they usually paid at the end of the month ... with the exception of the very last time he had a huge steaming bowl of Tomato Bisque.

Fortunately he went on to resume his very lucrative career, and no doubt he has totally forgot the $5.50 plus tax he owes The Godmother.

I like the idea that I am owed money by such a legend. I have had the pleasure of being there at an important time in their lives and knowing they enjoyed this soup so much makes it worth the debt...

WHAT DOES SHE DO WITH IT??

For the past twenty years, one customer has been buying two quarts weekly of Tomato Bisque. She uses it not only as a soup, hot and cold, but also as a salad dressing, to baste meats, chicken, fish, eggs and vegetables, she says.

It wouldn't surprise me if she washed her hair with it. Of course, I wouldn't suggest any of these uses except for what it was intended; 'SOUP'. Don't get too creative.

WHAT YOU EAT, YOU REAP...

She was a student at Pepperdine University, struggling financially to finish college. Her main meal of the day was Tomato Bisque soup as she trudged the happy road to graduation. When she could, she paid; when she couldn't, we figured it was our way of helping to insure that the future was full of promise with good kids like this.

You know the old saying, "what you give out, comes back a thousand times" and in this case it has.

Lora Kennedy, is currently vice president of feature casting for a major studio. We are proud of her. She's come a long way since her days at the Café eating bowls of Tomato Bisque.

She is mother to Orlando, a precious little boy. Lora, Marlys and I have 'invented' a terrific dessert call "Tiramisu on a Stick". We serve it at the Café and many of our catered events with rave reviews.

It has a U.S. government patent and we're hoping to get a quality ice-cream manufacturer to bring it to the marketplace so that the hordes can lick the stick with culinary joy and make it the next 'Krispy Kremes' phenomenon.

AND IT EVEN GETS STAR BILLING

Tomato Bisque took center stage at a gala wedding held May, 2005 for 200 plus guests, under the stars in Malibu.

Soup has never been the centerpiece dish for any of the weddings we catered. It's not "glamourous or gourmet" enough, most people think, but this groom was determined. He ate this soup practically every day as an undergraduate at Pepperdine University, and had his wedding menu planned for years.

Such a darling man, sweet, smart and quiet—the kind of guy every mother would want for her daughter. Probably brainwashed his bride from their first date about Tomato Bisque, and by the time I met her, she was hooked.

Daniele the lovely bride, is a very unusual and talented gal. She works in the film industry insuring that animals used in films are treated and cared for properly. She is the 'voice' of those without 'voices'.

Her kindness showed when she acquiesced to the grooms request, yet cleverly threw some grilled salmon and chicken into the menu, just in case some of the guests wanted more than soup. From the looks of the 'cleaned' bowls everyone seemed to fall under the Tomato Bisque spell.

THE OTHER SOUPS

In the fourteenth century, Venetians believed that soup would cure anything. In twentieth-century New York, in our strictly Jewish-Italian neighborhood, everyone, believed the Venetians were right.

Mrs. Rabiner, mother of one of my dearest buddies, Harvey, knew everyone who was sick in the neighborhood before even they did, and always had chicken soup ready. It didn't matter the ailment, you ate the soup and you got better. Forget the penicillin that cured the infection, or the surgery that took out the inflamed appendix. No way, it was the chicken soup that did it.

The ladies in the neighborhood swore that if we ate the chicken soup, we wouldn't get polio, which was a very big threat then. My grandma added, that if you wore garlic around your neck, you wouldn't get polio. What a funny little group of kids we were; always smelling of garlic and chicken soup. None of us ever got polio. How can you argure with that one.

Chicken soup and its cures have evolved into many different variations. Tomato Bisque is considered by many of our customers to be a close cousin to chicken soup's healing powers. We have Malibuites, who, finding it hard to walk without swaying after a hard day of surfing, eat a little Tomato Bisque and be on the next wave after licking the bowl.

We make the most delicious and unique soups ... unique because they all taste the way they are suppose to taste: pea soups tastes like peas, tortilla soup tastes like tortillias. Potato leek fills your mouth with the blend of sweet leeks and rich potatoes.

If you can boil water, I guarantee you can make chicken soup. A pot of water, some vegetables, especially unbruised celery, a couple of organic chickens, a little Godmother Mediterranean salt, some pepper, and always lots of tenderness. Lo and behold, sitting before you will be a delicious pipping hot bowl of soup. Maybe not like Mrs. Rabiner's, but one you made and that's mucho satisfying.

Soup is warm and comforting ... it is, the true comfort food. It makes you feel better even if you aren't sick. Soup nutures at a time when you might need the most nurturing. It wraps you in a warm snugly blanket as the first sip coats your throat.

Winter's in Malibu can get harsh ... yeah, you heard me, harsh. Certainly not like the Northeast or the Midwest, where fifty inches of snow is possible but we get our fair share of bone-chilling days, El Nino (lots and lots of rain) every ten years, fog every June, and a guarantee that Pacific Coast Highway will close at least once a year. Even the well-adjusted, can get frazzled and a large bowl of soup usually does the trick.

I am including a whole bunch of soup recipes, all original recipes, either dreamed by Marlys or created by our team. Even cold ones for those hot summer days.

The only time I remember to eat soup is when I'm sick. If I was smarter, I would eat soup more often. It's a great meal with few calories, and very satisfying, even without the warm bread and melted butter or better yet, olive oil.

THE SOUP PEOPLE...RADICAL, FREE AND INDEPENDENT

There are many stories about our 'soup people'. No other food item on our menu has that kind of loyalty and attention. My dilemma is how to include them all. I can't. So here are a few that are vivid in my memory because those involved were radical, free and independent Malibuites in their daily lives and shared the bond of a passion for our soups, too... How lucky can I be??

Philip and Amanda Dunne: Phillip who was twice nominated for an Academy Award had screenwriting credits that included *The Count of Monte Cristo*, *The Ghost and Mrs. Muir* (a favorite of mine) and *How Green Was My Valley* (another favorite). He also directed some classics like *Ten North Federick* and *Prince of Players*. He and Amanda, were members of that historical group of Hollywood illuminaries who dared to go to Washington in the '50's to protest the House Un-American Activities Committee because the committee's behavior was threatening the Constitution. Can you imagine?

Amanda, whose many talents included piloting her own plane, was always by his side with her brilliant mind and beautiful glow.

They enjoyed many many bowls of Tomato Bisque and Potato Leek soup at the shop or at their lovely home overlooking the blue Pacific. I cherished the time I spent with them both. I could never get enough of their reminiscing. Their tales of the film industry and their fight for freedom of speech and the democratic process still resonates in my ears. They're gone but never forgotten.

Mario Puzio, who wrote *The Godfather* novel and the screenplay for *The Godfather* movie receiving two Academy Awards for his glorious work, was a part-timer in Malibu during the summer, (always anxious for a bowl of Tomato Bisque). On one of his last visits, he presented me with a copy of his latest novel. *The Sicilian.* (How ironic ... read the chapter about my grandfather and Sicilians to know why). His inscription: "To The Godmother, a worthy note to the Godmother mystique with best wishes and thanks. Mario Puzio."

Mario and I had a great deal in common, short of course, of his magnificent writing talents. We were both from New York. He came from a much rougher neighborhood (Hell's Kitchen) than I did. The Bronx in comparison was like the French Riviera. But with our mutual Italian upbringing; blue collar families who ate pasta on Tuesdays, Thursdays and Sundays we were able to communicate the 'language of the old neighborhoods'. I sometimes reverted to a fan. I couldn't help myself. I asked him hundreds of questions about the writing of the book and the ultimate filming of that masterpiece, *The Godfather.* He was so generous with his time and answered as many questions as I threw at him.

It's the first and last time I have ever been proud of an Italian-American saga protrayed either on the big or small screen. It was perfection.

Cordelia Rodrick and her husband Harry were colorful characters besides being ferociously devoted to our bowls of soup. They were renegades; stanch believers in individual rights; the right to die your way, the right to protest, the right to free speech ... and free it was.

Cordelia, a very attractive woman, always beautifully coiffure, looked like a debutant and behaved with an ever present hippie mentality. She and Harry shared many a bowl of Tomato Bisque with another colorful character, Maxine Colby a long time Malibuite and talented local artist, whose daughter Erin was our first non-family employee.

In between the bowls of soup, if these characters weren't trying to proselytize any of their favorite causes, they were helping the homeless with clothing and food for the day and visiting the sick. They were always protesting whatever was necessary to protest at the time.

From the Malibu Colony came Tita Cooley. Courageously she walked, from Malibu to Washington, D.C. in the Great Peace March from March 1 to November 15, 1986 to protest the nuclear testing treaty. She carried containers of Tomato Bisque in her backpack. Most of it was gone before she reached Arizona. Joined on the trek somewhere along the road at different crossroads, were our beloved Mary Mac, her daughter Alicia, Ben and Hazel Berg, Cordelia and a few other unconventional Malibuites. They joined up with thousands on the outskirts of town and walked into Washington, to the White House, in total silence. One of those magical moments. Thousands from all walks of life moving silently through the streets of Washington and when they arrived at 1600 Pennsylvania Avenue, hung their shoes all over the gates surrounding the White House to symbolize their concerns.

I, so wanted to make that trip but somehow I found a thousand excuses. Some were legitimate, like who would run the Godmother while I was 'hiking', but in 1999, with that memory in mind, I asked Mary Mac if she would participate in the three-day Breast Cancer Walk from Santa Barbara to Malibu with me. She never hesitated.

That first year we walked 20 miles a day (total 80 miles) and slept in a two man tent each night. Mary Mac is narcoleptic. When she put her head to the floor of the tent, she was off in neverneverland. I, on the other hand, couldn't move because our bodies were stuck in this small area and thoughts about what I would do if I needed to use the 'facilities' during the night had to be immediately erased. First it was pitch black out there, and second, I couldn't move. I never Thank God, had to move. My Angels were watching over me.

The next five years, we participated in the event as volunteers. As 'seasoned and successful' walkers we got to drive the vans that picked up those walkers who couldn't finish the day. I loved that job a lot. We got to meet so many interesting people and our job was to make them feel proud, even if they only walked one block or twenty miles. One of the perks was that we didn't have to set-up a tent (which we never learned to do, someone usually felt sorry for us) because we slept in the van ... such luxury. Mary Mac was such a treasure to be with for three days.

All of these strong, independent people would have easily traveled by wagon train through fearful Indian territory to discover the West, or volunteered for the Civil War on either side. They are all extraordinary people and their common thread was our soups, especially Tomato Bisque.

TERAMO CELERY SOUP

INGREDIENTS:

2 cups celery, diced

1 small onion, diced

2 tbs. olive oil

¾ cup risotto rice, rinsed

1 tbs. tomato sauce

4 cups chicken stock, salted to taste

2 tbs. parsley, chopped

1 tsp. thyme

DIRECTIONS:

In a three quart soup pot, sauté the celery and onion in olive oil until soft (about 4 minutes). Stir in the risotto rice and coat with the olive oil mixture.

Pour in the chicken stock and the tomato sauce, plus the 1 teaspoon of thyme. Cook 30 minutes till the rice is cooked and creamy.

Stir in the chopped parsley just before serving.

Serve with freshly grated Parmesan Cheese.

SERVES 6

BEET and RED CABBAGE BORSCHT

INGREDIENTS:

2 potatoes, peeled, halved and thinly sliced

2 large or 3 small beets, peeled, halved and thinly sliced

4 cups vegetable broth

2 tbs. olive oil

1 medium yellow onion, chopped

1 carrot, peeled and diced

2 stalks celery, diced

2 cups red cabbage, chopped

½ cup tomato sauce

1 tbs. apple cider vinegar

1 tbs. honey

1 ½ tbs. fresh dill, chopped

½ tsp. course black pepper

Godmother salt to taste

DIRECTIONS:

In a medium pot, add the sliced potatoes, sliced beets and four cups of vegetable broth. Cover and cook for about 20 minutes.

In a saucepan, sauté in olive oil the chopped onion, diced carrots, diced celery and chopped red cabbage until they are tender (about fifteen minutes).

Add sautéed vegetables to potato-beet broth, along with the ½ cup of tomato sauce.

BEET and RED CABBAGE BORSCHT
(CONTINUED)

Add the black pepper, chopped dill, apple cider vinegar and honey to the pot. Simmer for 30 minutes or more.

Serve with a dollop of sour cream on top.

Serves 6

FRENCH ONION SOUP

INGREDIENTS:

2 medium shallots, minced

4 medium white onions, sliced and quartered

¼ cup butter, melted

4 cups chicken stock, salted to taste

½ cup Chablis wine

1 bay leaf

½ tsp. thyme

¼ tsp. black pepper

½ lb. provolone cheese, grated

¼ cup parmesan cheese, grated

6 slices French baguette, toasted

DIRECTIONS:

In a three quart soup pot, brown onions and shallots in butter until dark golden brown. Pour in Chablis and chicken stock, bring to a boil.

Lower to a simmer and add the bay leaf, thyme and black pepper. Simmer for 40 minutes.

Set out six medium soup bowls.

Place a toasted slice of french baguette into each soup bowl and divide the provolone and parmesan cheese between the six bowls. Ladle the hot soup on top of the bread and cheese.

Serves 6

TURKEY ORZO SOUP

INGREDIENTS:

4 medium carrots, peeled and chopped

6 stalks celery, diced

2 medium onions, diced

2 tbs. olive oil, to sauté

6 quarts turkey stock

1 lb. turkey breast, ½" cubes

Godmother salt and some pepper, to taste

1 cup orzo

½ cup parsley, finely chopped

½ cup grated parmesean cheese

DIRECTIONS:

In a ten quart soup pot, add the olive oil and the chopped carrots, celery and onion.

Sauté for 5 to 10 minutes until the vegetables are soft, but not browned. Add the 6 quarts of turkey stock and bring to a boil. Add the turkey and the orzo simmer for 30 minutes or until the orzo is tender. Stir in the finely diced parsley.

Sprinkle with grated parmesan cheese.

Serves 12

TUSCAN WHITE BEAN SOUP

INGREDIENTS:

½ lb. northern white beans, rinsed

1 medium ham hocks

3 tbs. olive oil

2 stalks celery

1 medium carrot, peeled and chopped

2 medium Roma tomatoes, chopped

4 cups chicken stock, salted to taste

1 bay leaf, crushed

1 tsp. lemon juice

DIRECTIONS:

Rinse and clean white beans and place in a bowl. Cover with water to soak overnight. Slice the skin on the ham hock on four sides and set aside.

In a four quart soup pot, sauté the garlic, onion, carrot and celery until soft (about 4 minutes). Pour in the chicken stock, add the drained northern white beans, the ham hock, chopped Roma tomatoes and the bay leaf.

Bring the soup to a boil and then turn down to a slow medium heat. Cook for 2 hours or until beans are tender.

Remove ham hock and let cool. Remove skin and meat of the bone, chop ham into medium-sized pieces.

TUSCAN WHITE BEAN SOUP
(CONTINUED)

Add the ham and the lemon juice to the pot, bring up to serving temperature.

Serve topped with crème fraiche and chopped chives.

Serves 6

SPLIT PEA SOUP

INGREDIENTS:

1 lb. green split peas

1 tbs. olive oil

1 medium yellow onion

2 carrots, peeled

3 stalks celery

6 cups vegetable broth

3 tsp. thyme

½ tsp. tarragon

1/8 tsp. cayenne pepper

Godmother salt to taste

DIRECTIONS:

Pick over dried split peas to remove gravel.* Rinse under cold water and set aside.

Place onion, carrots and celery in food processor, and chop until fine texture.

In a medium-size pot, add olive oil and finely chopped vegetables. Sauté over medium heat for fifteen minutes, stirring frequently.

Add one pound of green split peas, vegetable broth, thyme, tarragon and cayenne pepper.

Cook over medium heat until smooth and creamy (about 1 half to 2 hours).

SPLIT PEA SOUP
(CONTINUED)

* Gravel is 'always usually' present in peas and beans, when you purchase them.

Note: if more liquid is needed during cooking, add hot water or broth only.

Serves 6

MINESTRONE

INGREDIENTS:

2 tbs. olive oil

1 medium yellow onion, chopped

3 carrots, peeled and diced

4 stalks of celery, diced

1 medium zucchine, quartered lengthwise and sliced

3 potatoes, diced

8 Roma tomatoes, diced

½ cup white wine

3 cups beef broth

3 cups chicken broth

½ tsp. oregano

1 tsp. basil

2 bay leaves

¼ tsp. fine black pepper

Godmother salt to taste

DIRECTIONS:

In a medium soup pot, heat the olive oil, add chopped and diced onion, carrot, celery, zucchini and potatoes.

Stir until translucent, about 5 to 8 minutes. Then add the chicken broth and chopped tomatoes and bring to a boil.

MINESTRONE
(CONTINUED)

Add the fresh herbs, salt, peppers, and basil leaves. Lower heat to simmer and cook 30 to 40 minutes.

Serve with warm, crusty bread and grated parmesan cheese.

Serves 6

GINGER BUTTERNUT SQUASH SOUP

INGREDIENTS:

¼ cup butter, melted

1 small onion, finely chopped

1 tsp. ginger, fresh and grated

2 lbs. butternut squash, peeled and chopped

1 medium russet potato, peeled and chopped

2 cups chicken stock, salted to taste

½ cup cream

DIRECTIONS:

In a three quart heavy soup pot, sauté finely chopped onion and freshly grated ginger for about three minutes until soft and aromatic. Pour in the chicken stock and apple juice.

Add the peeled and choppd butternut squash and russet potato. Cover and cook over low heat for 40 minutes, until squash and potato are tender. Cool twenty minutes.

In a blender or food processor, blend in batches till smooth.

Pour batch into a soup pot, stir in cream and heat to serving temperature.

Serves 6

CURRIED CARROT SOUP

INGREDIENTS:

1 ½ lbs. carrot, peeled and chopped

3 tbs butter, melted

1 tsp. thyme, sauté

1 tbs. sugar

4 cups vegetable broth

½ cup basmati rice

1 tbs. butter, melted

1 tbs. curry powder, stir in butter

½ cup coconut milk, stirred in

DIRECTIONS:

In a medium soup pot, melt the butter and add the peeled and diced carrot and thyme, sauté until translucent, then add the sugar and stir.

Add the vegetable stock and basmati rice and bring to a boil.

Meanwhile, melt 1 tablespoon of butter in a small pan and then add the curry powder, stirring frequently till a paste forms.

Stir the curry paste into the boiling soup, lower heat to low and continue to cook for 30 minutes.

Remove from stove. When soup is partially cooled, puree in a food processor till smooth. Return to soup pot, add the coconut milk, and warm to serving temperature.

Serves 6

GAZPACHO

INGREDIENTS:

3 cups V-8 juice

2 cups beef broth

5 Roma tomatoes, seeded and diced

2 green onions, diced

2 cloves of garlic, minced

1 green bell pepper, diced

2 stalks of celery, diced

1 cucumber, peeled, seeded and diced

1 small jicama, peeld and diced

1 lemon, juice only

½ tsp. Worcestershire sauce

1 tsp. course black pepper

1 tbs. cilantro, chopped

1 tsp. cumin

Godmother salt to taste

DIRECTIONS:

In a two quart soup container, add V-8 juice, beef broth, juice of lemon, Worcestershire sauce and one teaspoon of cumin.

To the basic broth, add the diced and seeded tomatoes, diced green onions, minced garlic, diced green bell peppers, diced celery, the peeled, seeded and diced cucumber, and the peeled and diced jicama.

GAZPACHO
(CONTINUED)

Add the course black pepper and chopped cilantro. Stir well and chill 2 hours before serving.

*Seafood Gazpacho:

Same as the traditional gazpacho, but substitute

1 peeled and diced white radish instead of jicama

1 tbs. of chopped, fresh dill instead of cilantro

½ tsp. of Tabasco sauce instead of cumin

½ lb. of Bay shrimp

POTATO LEEK SOUP

INGREDIENTS:

3 tbs. butter, melted

3 large leeks, washed and chopped

3 medium white rose potatoes, peeled and cubed

2 small carrots, peeled and diced

3 tbs. flour

4 cups chicken broth

Godmother salt and some pepper to taste

DIRECTIONS:

In a medium soup pot, melt the butter and add the diced leeks, carrots and potatoes and stir frequently for 5 minutes.

Next, stir in the flour till the vegetables are well-coated, then add the chicken stock, salt and pepper, and continue to stir till broth thickens, about 8 to 12 minutes.

Lower heat to low and continue to simmer 20 to 30 minutes.

Serves 6

CREAMY VEGETABLE SOUP

INGREDIENTS:

1/3 cup butter, melted

1 ¼ large onion

5/8 bunch celery, chopped

2 3/8 medium carrots, peeled and chopped

2 3/8 medium potatoes, peeled and chopped

1 ¼ quarts vegetable or beef broth add to boiling broth

7/8 cup elbow macaroni

1 ¾ cup milk

5/8 cup cream

Godmother salt and some pepper to taste.

DIRECTIONS:

In a medium soup pot melt the butter and add the chopped onions, celery, carrots and potatoes, and sauté until just soft.

Then add the vegetable or beef broth, bring to a boil, lower to a medium heat and add the pasta. Continue to cook for 30 minutes, then add milk, cream and salt and pepper.

Continue to heat another 10 to 15 minutes. Do not let it boil.

Serves 6

TORTILLA SOUP

INGREDIENTS:

1 ½ tbs. olive oil, heated

1 tbs. garlic, minced

1 medium brown onion, finely chopped

2 stalks celery, finely chopped

2 medium carrots, peeled and diced

¾ quart chicken broth, added

1 ½ lbs. refried beans, stirred in

¼ tsp. black pepper, freshly ground

1 dash cayenne

1 ½ tbs. cumin

1 ½ tbs. chili powder

1 ½ cups, canned Italian tomatoes, pureed

2 oz. cheddar cheese, shredded

2 oz. jack cheese, shredded

½ cup sour cream, stirred in

¼ bunch cilantro, chopped

DIRECTIONS:

In a medium soup pot, heat the olive oil and add the garlic, diced onion, celery and carrots. Sauté until soft.

Then add the chicken stock, refried beans, pureed tomatoes, and the spices—black pepper, cayenne, cumin and chili powder. Bring to a boil, then lower to simmer and continue cooking for 40 minutes.

TORTILLA SOUP
(CONTINUED)

Remove from heat and stir in shredded jack and cheddar cheese, sour cream and chopped cilantro.

Serves 8.

1 hour

NEW ENGLAND CLAM CHOWDER

INGREDIENTS:

3 tbs. butter

1 medium onion, peeled and chopped

3 stalks celery, diced

2 small white potatoes, peeled and diced

2 small carrots, peeled and diced

½ small green bell pepper, diced

3 tbs. flour, stirred in

3 cups chicken broth

1 cup cream

27 oz. chopped clams, drained

1 tbs. sherry, dry

½ tsp. thyme, dried

¼ tsp. tarragon, dried

2 tsp. Worcestershire sauce

3 dashes Tabasco sauce

Godmother salt and some pepper to taste

DIRECTIONS:

In a medium soup pot, melt the butter and sauté the vegetables till translucent, about 5 to 8 minutes.

Add the flour and stir till all the vegetables are well coated.

Then add the liquid from the drained clams, (reserving the clams till later), the chicken broth and the cream and bring to a boil.

NEW ENGLAND CLAM CHOWDER
(CONTINUED)

Lower heat to simmer and add the thyme, tarragon, Worcestershire and Tabasco sauce. Let simmer for 30 to 40 minutes.

Remove from heat, stir in the clams and let the soup sit for 5 to 10 minutes. Add salt and pepper to taste.

Serves 6.

MUSHROOM SOUP

INGREDIENTS:

16 oz. mushrooms, thinly sliced

1 cup leeks, chopped

6 cups vegetable or chicken stock

¼ cup butter

½ cup tomato sauce

¼ cup water

¼ cup arrowroot

½ tsp. oregano

½ tsp. freshly grounded black pepper.

Godmother salt to taste

DIRECTIONS:

In a 4 quart saucepan, melt butter, add the chopped leaks, and cook 5 minutes or until soft. Add mushrooms, sauté another 5 minutes. Add to tomato sauce, stock, oregano and black pepper. Simmer thirty minutes.

Stir ¼ arrowroot into ¼ cup of water, stir until well dissolved, add to mushroom soup, stirring constantly until soup is thick and velvety.

Salt to taste then serve.

6 Servings

MAHATTAN CLAM CHOWDER

INGREDIENTS:

3 tbs. olive oil

1 tsp. chopped garlic

2 stalks celery, diced

2 carrots, peeled and diced

1 small green bell pepper, diced

1 ear corn, remove kernels from cob

3 medium red potatoes, sliced

6 Roma tomatoes, seeded and chopped

½ cup tomato sauce

6 cups vegetable broth

½ tsp. oregano

½ tsp. cumin

½ tsp. black pepper

3 tbs. parsley, chopped

3 tbs. cilantro, chopped

1 lb. fresh clams (out of shells) or

2 cans of 7 oz. chopped clams

Godmother salt to taste

DIRECTIONS:

In a four quart saucepan, pour olive oil, diced celery, carrots, green bell pepper, and garlic ... sauté over medium heat five minutes.

MANHATTAN CLAM CHOWDER
(CONTINUED)

Add vegetable broth, tomato sauce, chopped tomatoes, fresh corn and diced red tomatoes. Cook over medium heat till reaches a boil, lower heat to a simmer.

Add oregano, cumin, black pepper and salt to taste. Simmer 40 minutes.

Just before serving, add chopped clams, parsley and cilantro and simmer 8 minutes.

Serve with butter crusty bread.

6 servings

LENTIL SPINACH SOUP

INGREDIENTS:

2 tbs. olive oil

1 medium onion, diced

2 cloves garlic, minced

2 small carrots, peeled and chopped

2 stalks celery, diced

2 cups lentil, washed

4 cups vegetable broth

2 cups peeled Roma tomatoes, chopped

2 tbs. molasses

1 tbs. thyme, fresh, chopped

½ cup red wine

2 cups spinach, washed and chopped

Godmother salt and some black pepper to taste

DIRECTIONS:

In a medium soup pot heat the olive oil, add onion, garlic, carrots, celery and lentils, sauté for six to ten minutes. Add vegetable broth, chopped Roma tomatoes and wine, bring to a boil.

Add the molasses, chopped thyme and salt and pepper to taste.

Simmer 20 minutes, add the washed chopped spinach, simmer 15 to 20 minutes.

6 servings

HOT AND SOUR SOUP

INGREDIENTS:

4 dry Chinese mushrooms

2 tbs. dry tree ears*

14 dry tiger lilies*

½ lb. bean curd

1 scallion, chopped

4 oz. bamboo shoots, shredded

¼ cup cooked pork or chicken

2 eggs, beaten

2 tbs. cornstarch and 4 tsp. water mixed together

4 cups chicken broth

1 tbs. soy sauce

pepper to taste

2 tbs. wine vinegar

1 tbs. sesame oil

DIRECTIONS:

Snap stems off Chinese mushrooms and place mushrooms, tree ears, tiger lilies in a bowl.

Pour 1 ½ cups boiling water over mushrooms, and let soak 15 minutes. Drain.

Heat broth and add bean curd, tiger lilies, scallions, pork or chicken, simmer 2 minutes. Add pepper, vinegar and cornstarch. When thick, add eggs and stir constantly.

Serve immediately. 6 servings.

* can be purchased at gourmet food shops or chinese markets.

part three

DRAMA AT ITS FINEST

Weddings are theater at its best. The plots make for the best of drama. As I look back over the many years we've catered weddings, I realize, how many of these wedding events were unforgettable and will always be part of our Godmother memories. Hundreds of stories, funny, emotional, stressful; so much advice and information that it will take another book the size of the Bible to spell it all out for you ... I'd swim with snakes in the Ganges, rather than attempt another book now. But I will share some of what I've learned and hopefully give some helpful advice.

If you want an original wedding; one where your style and signature is all over it, please don't get taken in by the wedding "marketeers" ... those whose sole purpose is to make money. If my sole purpose was to make money I'd been living in Italy eating white figs and proscuito by now ... and The Godmother would be but a few good memories for some. Our purpose is to insure that we are doing something creative and challenging and that the end results are perfect. Perfect is tough but it's the only way for us. Don't buy hundreds of magazines and wedding books ... they all say the same thing in different ways ... one or two will do. Of course you want to design a wedding which reflects you both, something personal and intimate. Listen to everyone's suggestions, if you must, but always remember this is not everyone's weddings, it's yours. Take what you need of the information you'll receive in truck loads and throw out the rest.

Weddings are so much fun and so very challenging for us because we get to create the dream wedding for the bride and groom from the tasty appetizers of white bean and rosemary bruschetta and mini beef filet with our own horseradish to jumbo cup cakes filled with luscious, mouth-watering chocolate.

We hold our breath while we search for Bud, the retreat dog before he has a chance to attack the wedding cake with his wide paws. We treat each wedding event as if it's the first we've ever done. We dot every eye and then some. We become a part of the family. Such a magical day for the couple. Dreams of the perfect wedding bounce in the brides head. We make those dreams come true.

First the stories about the people who actually experienced the experience then the 'tips'. Anything more will freeze your brain and stress you beyond recovery.

ONCE UPON A TIME....

The many couples who have crossed our threshold are usually getting married for the first time; some the second, but only one bride did it three times ... and we were there each time ... this is that story.

It began in the 1990's when she first hired us to cater her first wedding.

The she of this story is an elegant, disciplined, intelligent, talented actress and the wedding was to be at her home in the Serra Retreat area of Malibu. It was a large, yet warm and comfortable home, overlooking the creek; a charming and romantic spot that was the perfect setting for both the ceremony and the reception.

The groom, handsomely dashing and charming, a delightfully engaging young man seemed thrilled and very much in love.

Her parents arrived from the Midwest, dressed in their finest "going to church" clothes, carrying mouth-watering cookies and cheeses from Wisconsin, sausages from Illinois and cream puffs from Minnesota. A long standing custom for this family was to bring food to the wedding table, to add to the wedding feast.

The Wedding Feast...

Antipasto

Assorted Grilled Tomato Crostini

Coconut Shrimp

Vegetable Kabobs

Cheese Basket
w/Olives/Dates/Fruits

Buffet

Rosemary Grilled Chicken on Red Pepper Sauce

Beef Tenderloin with Portabello Mushrooms

Wasabi Mashed Potatoes

Steamed Asparagus

Spinach Salad with Gorgonzola and Spicy Pecans

Assorted Grilled Foccacia Breads

Chocolate & Carrot Cake Cupcakes

Assortments of cheeses, sausages, cream puffs

And cookies!!!!!!!!

The day was alive with such positive energy. The guests appeared to be a very loving group of people, I thought, as I drove home that evening.

A year later, practically to the date, the bride called and said she was getting married.. The word *again*, never entered her vocabulary or mine. "It will be at my home," she said, "and I just want to make some adjustments to that wonderful menu you served last time."

There was a brief moment of uncomfortable silence as I swallowed hard and continued the conversation.

So back from the Midwest come her parents, same treats under their arms: cookies, sausages, cream puffs and Wisconsin cheese.

The only thing different from wedding number one, was the groom, his family and friends.

When I heard from my "bride" again two years later, I wasn't worried ... I was sure she was looking for a party for the holidays because we had met a few times during the past two years and she appeared happy. This was the holiday season, after all.

How wrong I was! "Could you do a small event for me on December 8th at my home?" she asked.

"Sure", I replied, "any theme to the event?"

"Yes", came the reply, "I'm getting married." I nearly fell off of my chair, but the cool professional I am didn't give me away, even when I blurted out "What?"

"I'm getting married" she repeated.

"Holy shit," I said quietly.

Why I didn't say *NO, NO, NO...I'm not going to face your parents again*, I don't know. Maybe it's because my curiosity got the best of me and I couldn't resist meeting the third groom and his family and friends. Or maybe, although I could never use names, it would make a good story someday. I honestly don't know what possessed me except I did like her a lot. So here we go again.

The parents, decked out in new clothes and looking somewhat bewildered, arrived with their cookies, cheese, cream puffs and sausages. They were simple, unsophisticated folk who must have thought Los Angeles was like landing on the moon, with Malibu filled with all those "strange aliens". They seemed resigned that possibly everyone in Malibu married three times. I was probably the only one looking carefully at people to see if there was any reaction, especially from the brides side of the family ... they've been here before, and there wasn't even a look of genteel uneasiness.

After the ceremony, the groom made a particular effort to circulate throughout the room, graciously greeting and kissing everyone. He was so very happy. "Enjoy the moment, for you too, will probably pass," crossed my mind throughout the evening.

I must say that my friend, the bride, had excellent taste in men. All of her grooms were good-looking, charming, rich, intelligent, and possessing incredible manners.

At the end of the evening, as I was packing up our pots, I hugged her parents, who at this point, were practically family to me, and moved towards the front door. I wasn't fast enough. The bride screamed and ran across the room, jumping on me with a huge bear hug and nearly throwing us to the floor. I hugged back and whispered into her ear, "I like you a lot, but don't call me if this one doesn't work." She seemed startled, at first, by my comment and hugged me again, saying, "No problem, this is the one."

If she was nuts to go for number four, she'd have to go to the 'Yellow Pages' for help. I was officially retired for this particular bride.

I've talked to her often these past several years. All is well and happy. In fact, we just did a lovely sit-down dinner party for thirty in honor of her birthday.

Gives you hope that if something doesn't work, just keep trying until it does.

THE GODMOTHER TAKES THE FALL...

When Annamarie and Matt fell in love, they spent a great deal of time visiting the Serra Retreat. As a surprise, Matt presented Annamarie with a beautiful engagement ring at the Retreat one summer evening. They felt it was predestined to have their wedding there.

We had only a few available dates; they quickly picked one and off we were to the planning stages. Contracts were signed and sealed.

Two months later, Matt calls and rather sheepishly asks if I would do them a huge favor. I like them so very much that nothing they ask could be difficult (I thought). "Could I write a letter directed to them, Annamarie and Matt, a nasty letter in fact, stating that the date of their marriage at the Retreat could not be changed under any circumstance?" The letter needed to be unequivocal in it's intent.

Matt's sister was also getting married (and picked the date first) a week before Matt and Annamarie's wedding date at the Serra Retreat. The family would have to then travel twice within a week, from New York to Los Angeles to attend both weddings. His sister wasn't happy unless the date at the retreat could be changed real fast, a family crisis would erupt. If I would agree to be the "bad guy," they could avert a major blow-up. Matt with his sweet, charming personality convinced me to write the "nasty" letter. It really wouldn't be a lie, because we couldn't change the date, not to anything that they wanted anyway. It was the "nasty" part that was a bit of a stretch.

With great trepidation, I agreed. I was really frustrated because I didn't want to meet Matt's family and have them dispise me with our first hellos ... but we needed to get this resolved. I wrote the letter.

The Angels were watching over us again. Matt's sister changed her date because of another scheduling problem and they didn't have to show the letter to anyone.

When I met the parents, it was all love and kisses. They had no clue how close they came to "not speaking to that unreasonable woman" ... me.

Weddings are emotional roller coasters that could give you the ride of a lifetime or scare the hell out of you ... It's up to you.

In California, where anything is possible, you can make over $300,000 and not be able to afford a home, you and your dog probably have therapists, your hairdresser is straight, your plumber is gay, the woman who delivers FedEx is into S&M, and your Mary Kay cosmetics rep is a guy in drag. Anything goes in this state but it is possible to have a wonderful wedding.

This is the time when both bride and groom should share the decision-making process ... not after the wedding. It's the time to determine if you both can live with each other's decisions. Do you like her tastes? Do you think he's too passive? Do you both understand the culture you're getting into? The answers to some of these questions can avert many problems down the road.

THE BRIDE WAS PERFECTLY 'CAST'

It was obvious to anyone who has spent more than five minutes with Jose and Grace that they were a perfect match. They had known each other for about a year before they chose the Retreat for their ceremony and reception.

Jose was a big six feet three inches tall, good looking, young man, born in Venezuela and educated at UCLA. Grace was a dainty little soul, born into an Irish-Catholic family in Los Angeles. All of Jose's family, totaling more than fifty people, were making the trip with his mother to Los Angeles, most of them for the first time.

It was going to be a glorious affair: Spanish guitars, multi-cultural menu, colorful costumes.

The night before the wedding, as they were discussing the wedding ceremony, Momma casually said "Tomorrow, as we are walking down the aisle, I would like the organist to play my late husband's favorite song."

The bride was shocked. She had no idea that Jose was walking down the aisle with his mother. Was this before her? After her or what? A little, unknown South American custom not mentioned ...

A lot of screaming began, all in Spanish, with nasty looks and hands flying everywhere. Jose tried unsuccessfully to stop his mother and Grace, from yelling at each other. He was deathly afraid they might start swinging, and then this would never be resolved. So he stepped in between them, and in doing so, inadvertently pushed Grace against the large television set in the hotel room, she broke her left arm.

On the day of the wedding, as is my usual custom, I headed toward the Terance Room, which is the bride's dressing room, to spend a few minutes with Grace before she walked down the aisle. When I popped my head in the door, she was crying, fully clothed in her wedding dress, a huge 'cast' on her arm, and surrounded by her bridesmaids. When she saw me, she screamed "Godmother, I'm not getting married today." "Oh, boy," I said, having no other intelligent thought for the moment. Of course, my initial thought is always about the food. "What the hell are we going to do with 125 beef tenderloins?" went through my head.

After taking a very deep breath, I asked everyone to clear the room. I sat next to Grace and preceded to listen to her story. Her bridesmaids were no help. They kept telling her that 'if he abuses you now, he will always abuse you.' That's possible but there is no way Jose (sorry for the rhyme) abused her. It was an unfortunate accident. This is where my sound intuition comes in handy. I'd spent six months with these two. I know them fairly well … enough to stake my last buck on a nonviolent Jose and his love for Grace.

But I decided to go look for him, and found him down near the gardens, totally unaware that his fate was being decided this very minute by a bunch of hysterical women.

He was indeed trying to prevent a volatile scene occurring last night between these two emotionally charged women. It was a terrible accident and he was so sorry to have been responsible for any pain and discomfort to his "beautiful Grace". He realized that he should have told Grace about this little custom sooner, but he was scared because he knew she wouldn't be very happy with it. Of course, not knowing, she was definitely furious. Trust me, always choose not happy over furious.

"Marry this young man and be happy the rest of your life." Your accident was indeed an accident. He would never hurt you." I told Grace when I returned to the Terance Room.

Cultural differences are difficult in themselves, so patience and understanding are needed, and definitely talk about everything … especially little odd ball cultural customs.

Respect is essential. It's the fabric of how you function in a sound, happy, and stable relationship. Love isn't enough.

Their wedding went off without a hitch. The bride was beaming, the groom was proud. They called me several months later, to thank me again. They were at the airport on their way to Venezuela, where Momma was throwing them yet another wedding reception. They check in yearly; and they are still madly in love and learning to respect each other's space on a daily basis.

THE 'GOD' TIPS...

1. ALWAYS REMEMBER TO BREATHE.

2.. LISTEN AND THEN FILTER.

When you agreed to walk down life's path together, you automatically became fair game for everyone; well-meaning friends, loving family and the "wedding marketeers". You'll be shocked to discover how many people think they know how to put on a wedding. Listen and filter. Take what you need, throw out the rest. Just keep repeating to yourself that this is your wedding and you are in control. Character defects, control issues and egos will blast out of you from every corner of your life. Don't panic. Everyone goes through this stage. The Bride and Groom must be strong and maintain a calm state at all times. KEEP REPEATING ... this is OUR wedding. It doesn't matter who is paying for it either. If there are "strings" like you don't get to decide the number of guests who should attend, the menu choices, or the type of music, find another way to get it done. Unfortunately, many weddings are designed to make "others" happy. Never do ' happy for others before you do happy for you'. This is the only day besides your birthdays, that will forever be yours.

3. FIND A CATERER who is passionate about food. Make the food quality a priority. You may have convinced yourselves that guest accept wedding invitations because of you ... Wrong!!!!!! A lot of surveys are done yearly and most people who have attended more than one wedding consider this particular event a big bore and attend out of obligation to someone in the family, including the bride and groom. Apparently the real reason they come is for a good meal,

(of course I'm prejudiced on this matter) good music, to possibly meet a life partner and have a happy time. Many weddings are orchestrated with long periods of waiting for the production to begin; the first dance, the bride dances with her dad, the groom dances with his mom, speeches from everyone that's ever known them from age two to present day and then to cap it off, small talk around the table with a bunch of people you don't know and wouldn't want to either. You can change all that by serving an outstanding meal, not necessarily expensive but carefully selected and then insuring that everyone laughs a lot by throwing 'routine' and 'tradition' out the window. Incidentally, you must like and trust your caterer.

4. HIRE A PROFESSIONAL WEDDING COORDINATOR. Not someone who might volunteer from your family or friends. This is the person you really have to like or at least respect for the next several months. You'll be spending a great deal of time together. This person MUST have a sense of humor or she/he should be in another profession. This person should be your own angel who will hold your hand until the minute you let go and take each other's.

5. BE COURAGEOUS ... unless you can afford the costs of a full on wedding don't do it and don't let your parents or friends do it for you. Don't feel pressured or embarrassed. What is important here is the choice you made to be together for the rest of your lives. If you had too, you could take your wedding vows under an oak tree in the park and serve ice tea and chocolate-covered cream puffs to your guests. It's that simple. You're guests will love it ... and you'll still have a few bucks left over for the honeymoon.

THE BRIDES, THE GROOMS, THE MOM'S AND DAD'S

"That wedding day is etched in my memory! The Godmother and her food were one of the high points (and there weren't many). She was so helpful in picking out what to serve and in taking care of everything food related. She took a big weight off of me. (Now, if she could've done something with David's family, that would've been quite an accomplishment). She made a lot go smoothly and made our guests feel comfortable and welcomed. The food was delicious, but it's been almost 22 years, so I can't remember the details. Mostly, I remember her happy face and her enthusiasm, and that The Godmother and the food were a great addition to our wedding."

—David and Barbara Lampert, 1984

"Danielle and I were married at the Admason house in Malibu. The staff there recommended the Godmother of Malibu to handle our reception.

Our first impression after meeting her is that you'd be foolish not to trust her. We knew we could leave the entire event in her capable hands.

The Godmother put together an amazing vegetarian menu. From the ample portions there were no leftovers. The meal and its presentation were perfectly matched to the celebration we wanted our wedding to be. And Dolores was there the whole time to make sure we were happy. Our friends' then-four-year-old daughter gave the rave review, "that was the best party I've ever been to!" That goes double for us.

Beyond the delicious food, there's an intangible element to Dolores' creations. She is in there; the Godmother takes care of you."

—Bill Dawson & Danielle Good July, 1996

<u>FROM THE BRIDE</u>

"Everyone knows Dolores can cook, but how does her food get transfigured and become divine? After years of study, I have finally figured out what makes Dolores the Godmother of all caterers: it is the love and attitude that goes into every stir and sauté.

The first time my future husband and I met Dolores, we had already been to a few other caterers. Each of them had sat us down and regaled us with a tasting menu. The choices to be made were endless: soup or salad, walking, seated, canapes or canopies, cream-based or consumme, and how much time did we want to leave for the receiving line? 35 minutes or 37 1/2? Inevitably, we felt overwhelmed by our catering research. We'd drive home jittering from the seven different cakes we'd sampled and wonder whether we were up to this very complex task of getting married.

When we met with Dolores, she put a cup of her creamy, fantastic Tomato Bisque Soup in front of each of us and got down to business. She wanted to know who was marrying us. We asked about the 'tasting menu.' She looked at us funny for a second and then gestured towards our empty soup bowls. "You just had it." And with that, my husband and I knew we had found the caterer of our dreams. Not only was her bisque the best soup we'd ever tasted, but with Dolores in our camp, my husband and I were free to stop obsessing on napkins and encouraged to spend a second or two thinking about spending the rest of our lives together.

Like an experienced coach, Dolores worked that wedding into a state of perfection and made it all feel effortless. The appearance of drinks and asparagus crepes at just the right moment happened with the same ease and naturalness as the setting of the sun over the Pacific. Over six years later, we still hear about the Grilled Beef with Wasabi Horseradish Cream Sauce! Weeks after the wedding, I did wonder how Dolores got all those delicacies and cutlery and a dance floor out to the tip of a point over Malibu. But at the time, we all just reveled in perfect joy under the stars in our finery. And that is what makes Dolores' food beyond compare: the joy and love is cooked right in and no recipe book can tell you how to do that. Dolores herself is the secret ingredient that you must experience if you are to have any event involving food raised to the level of the sublime.

In closing, I must devote a few words to the 'attitude' referenced above. On our honeymoon, we learned that our insane florist had physically threatened my mother wielding dozens of violet nosegays. Dolores dispatched all 250 pounds of him without a blink, and that was just one of several close calls that never interrupted our evening. Dolores' charming practicality easily outwits and overpowers any fiesty vendor and cuts away all unnecessary hassles in event planning. And her first question to us ("who is marrying you?") led us to a wonderful pastor and a new parish we've called home since our wedding. As Catholics who had decided not to use our local church for our wedding, we had been unable to find a priest to do the job until Dolores introduced us to her friend Fr. Bill Kerze, who has now not only married us but baptized our children. Where would we be without Dolores? We celebrate every Mother's Day with her and we've even borrowed her home in Hawaii for a vacation. Our parents, our kids, we all unite in proclaiming: "Dolores rocks!" It began with food and somehow it ends there too.

As I sit here writing this, thinking about how much I adore Dolores, the creaminess of that bisque with just a hint of dill and all those other esoteric ingredients impossible to fit between the covers of any book are conjured up, and it's all I can do to not jump in my car and drive to Malibu for soup and a joyous hello."

—Lizzy Bentley O'Neal/Arge O'Neal, September, 1998

FROM MOM AND DAD....

"Our daughter had always been our princess, so when she said she wanted to get married, we knew the day had to be perfect for her. She began searching the Internet and found a few locations in the Malibu area. While driving, in search of the castle (yes, there was a castle—fitting for a princess), they took a wrong turn...or was it the right turn? They found themselves at the Serra Retreat. They knew immediately they had found their wedding location.

We were then invited to tour the grounds with the Godmother of Malibu. It was a spectacular Retreat house, and she was a very charming lady. Our son-in-law is a surfer, so being able to see the ocean from the point at the Retreat was very meaningful. The flowers were in bloom, the trees brought shade and peace, the fountains, the chapel and the point were all too good to be true. We were overwhelmed with the Spanish architecture, colors, multiple levels of the grounds and the overall tranquility we felt.

The date was chosen and the fun began—yes, the fun!! We decided to have The Godmother cater and coordinate our special day (the best decision we made in months). We met several times and got to sample some of her wonderful hors d'oeuvres and finalize the plans. Everything was arranged and in the Godmother's hands. Since the wedding was in September, we were concerned with the possibility of rain. She informed us that in all the years she's been coordinating and catering, it had never rained on her parade.

When the day arrived, the weather was beautiful, the chapel wedding was blessed, and there they were—Mr. & Mrs. Matthew Fagundes. It was time to party.

The bride and groom descended to the point as the guests sprinkled lavender petals on them like rain. At the point, we had champagne toasts and delicious hors d'oeuvres. What a beginning!

The staff made sure everyone had both food and drink. The ocean view was beautiful and we could even see the castle that was once in our plans. After the cocktail hour, the guests moved down the beautiful Spanish steps towards the dinner area which was set with white linen tables, enveloped by white umbrellas. Dinner was outstanding and abundant. The cake from "The Bread Basket" was exquisite and ended our magical day.

We could never have coordinated the set-up, clean-up, staff and dinner for the entire day. We actually enjoyed every second of our family and friends because we found The Godmother, who attended to every detail so that our princess could have her perfect day.

Four years later we still receive compliments from those who attended. They mention the great time they had at our daughter's wedding. What more could we have asked for? Nothing."

—Don & Vonnie Turkal, 2001

_____

SECOND TIME AROUND...

"When I met Dolores, I instantly knew my fiance and I had found our perfect match for our wedding reception dinner, which was held at Malibu's glorious Serra Retreat. Maybe it was her disarming gorgeous smile; maybe it was her easy and robust laugh; maybe it was her irreverence and no nonsense; or maybe it was that attitudinal

312

swagger that's her special brand of self-assurance. My beloved was sold when he asked whether she accepted American Express and she responded, "What, are you crazy?" Actually, for me it was her salt-of-the-earth authenticity and mamma-bear warmth. ....and of course, her incredible delicious food at her Godmother Café.

In a time of frilly things and fussy details and professionals who can be equally fussy and frilly (not to mention opportunistic and greedy), we lucked out!!! It was refreshing to find someone so talented and well-organized yet genuine, patient and kind. That's Dolores. She's a great combo plate herself.

I was an older, self-sufficient bride and my mother lived across the country, unable to participate in the planning. My future mother-in-law was ailing and unable to participate as well. I hadn't realized how starved I was for that inimitable nurturing force of a mother-figure in the midst of it all. But when you're frazzled and confused, what is more comforting than a mother's attention, assurances, protection and love? It just doesn't get better.

Thanks to Dolores, I had peace of mind. I felt not only total assurance that the reception dinner would be delicious and that her staff would be impeccably polite to our guests, but also I felt I could run to her and complain and fret freely. She was my shelter from the tempest of my own frayed nerves...which are the priviledge and price of planning one's own life-long dream wedding.

In fact our wedding surpassed any dream I'd dared to hope for!"

—Meredith Muncy, Lucky, lucky bride of John Whelpley, March, 2001

———————————————————

313

FROM THE GROOM....

"When I first met Denise, my bride, the first thing that popped into my head was "Boy, am I in trouble.". To give you a clue of what kind of person my wife, is cross Marie Antoinette with Cat Woman and I think you got it. She's Italian and I'm Irish..Give me a beer and a television set showing a ball game and I am as happy as a pig in you know what. She is much more colorful and demanding than I ....She's only calm when she's asleep.

I don't know about the Humphrey Bogart line regarding the makings of a beautiful relationship because we already have that.

It is a blessing to have met and married my wife Denise.

Our wedding day was so very special because of Dolores and her staff at the Godmother. The food was divine, making the Italians from the East Coast especially happy and content. The East Coast crowd doesn't think anyone on the West Coast can cook. The Godmother proved them very wrong.

The memory of that day is etched into our minds for the rest of our lives...Before we met Dolores, I was pushing for eloping for many different reasons, the biggest being the fact that the stress of planning one's own wedding is tremendous and makes you wonder why in God's name you are doing it in the first place.

The test we both endured and came through with a new found love and affection for each other. We are ecstatic we married at Serra Retreat and we owe it all to Dolores.

The day was outstanding and we love you for the joy you brought into our lives."

—Timothy Ryan (Denise)
May, 2005

(Tim & Denise presented me with a beautiful gold Angel they bought in Rome. I cherish their gift. How did they know my connection with Angels?...)

FROM AN "ARCHED RIVAL"... THE DAD

This call was received from David Devine, father of the bride Kate Devine, who had just married Mark Brady at the Serra Retreat on October 2nd, 2005. David, it was revealed in previous conversations, is a Boston Red Sox fan, but we managed to keep that subject out of the wedding planning, until...THIS PHONE CALL...

"Hello to the Godmother. This is David Devine, Kate's dad, and I wanted you to know how pleased and honored we were to be associated with you and your endeavors at the wedding. It was absolutely 110%, 10% more than I had expected. It was flawless, you did a great job.

"I almost feel like rooting for the Yankees tonight, but my father would turn over in his grave, so let's leave it that whoever wins deserves to play Chicago.

"Back to the wedding, it was a memorable experience. Thank you so very very much."

—David Devine, October, 2005

A GLORIOUS ARGENTINA GALA

"You gave our darling Lauren and our wonderful Gonz, a wedding they will never forget. It was perfect.

Muchas Gracious".....

—Kevin & Anne Fitzpatrick, September, 2006

"Hi Dolores

It was the MOST BEAUTIFUL WEDDING I have ever seen!!!! I am still in a state of shock! The setting was glorious and the food was great. All the guests were astounded by the beauty and everyone had a wonderful time. The staff was great and everything ran so smoothly. i could not have dreamed that it would be so magical. I couldn't be happier".

Sharon MacDuffee, brides mother

OCTOBER, 2007

Dear Dolores, et al.

First thank you all so much for making our wedding everything we could have ever hoped for! Everything was absolutely exquisite and all of our friends and family truly enjoyed the celebration. You are each the best at what you do and it was wonderful to work with such talented professionals.

You made our wedding day one of the best days of our lives!

Veronica Feewald and Raphael Aguirre
Serra Retreat

AND SO

As you know by now, weddings are stressful, intriguing and frustrating, each so different and yet so similar but they are glorious experiences for us because we get to use our imaginations and design a memorable day filled with festive activities and luscious foods for the wedding couple, their family and friends.

We understand what each couple wants and we make it all happen. We make dreams come true. For these many experiences, for our many friends, for the hundreds of roads we traveled with them, we feel very fortunate.

part four

Thank You All

Hundreds and hundreds more thank yous fill boxes all over the Godmother; in closets at my home; on shelves in the garage. Eloquently worded and beautifully expressed notes of appreciation thanking us for fulfilling dreams and bringing happiness to so many at such important times in their lives. I wish we could have published them all.

I read them every so often to remind myself, especially when my back is aching and my knees bounce like Jell-o, why I continue on year after year. This works far better than any physical therapy, surgery or medication. It's pure magic or better yet, it's those Angels watching over us.

The road from the Bronx to Malibu was a long journey. I followed my own dream supported with the words of Maria Callas "who envisioned the road, surveyed it and bulldozed it into actuality" whose legacy taught me to do the same.

From so many in my life I've learned a work ethic; a discipline to try and do the very best I could do and never give up on a dream.

My Mom, Marlys, Valerie, Duane, my family, my friends and those Angels (Maria Callas, of course, too), kept pushing me up the hills around the many twists, bumps, delays and short detours to emerge with such gratitude.

I did what I set out to do. I hope my legacy will be that I brought an awareness of good food to this part of the world and I did it 'my way'. The Godmother showed people the difference. And for that I feel blessed.

'Arrivederci ad un altro giorno'

POST SCRIPT.......

My beautiful Sophia who was either under, beside or some where near my desk, while I labored over this book these past ten years, left this earth for the Rainbow Bridge on June 6, 2007. I would never had the tenacity to keep going without her huge brown eyes looking up at me at my most frustrated moments and saying with those sweet and caring "eye-liner eyes" "it's ok, just do it". My wish is that all of us leave this earth as she did ... at the dog age of 105, lying in her favorite petunias, and dreaming of juicy rib eye...

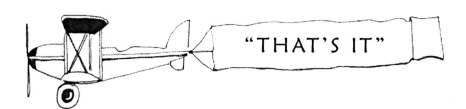

Printed in the United States
95582LV00004B/217-261/A